Michael W. Fox born in England and now living in Golden Valley, Minnesota, USA, is a veterinarian with a PhD degree in medicine and a Doctor of Science degree in ethology/animal behavior from the University of London, England. He is a Member of the Royal College of Veterinary Surgeons, member of the British Veterinary Association, Honor Roll Member of the American Veterinary Medical Association, long-time member of the American Holistic Veterinary Medical Association, and founding member of the International Association for Applied Animal Ethology. He helped make animal behavior and animal welfare science part of the veterinary teaching curriculum around the world, and more generally awakening public sensibility through his internationally syndicated newspaper column *Animal Doctor* both in the U.S. and in many other countries. He has authored over 50 books, including award-winning children's fiction, and is an advocate of reverence for life and One Health.

His website is *www.drfoxonehealth.com*

Books by the Author:
One Health: Veterinary and Ethical Perspectives. Taylor and Francis Group LLC, London and New York, 2025.
Healing Animals and the Vision of One Health. (2011). CreateSpace Publ/Amazon.com
Animals & Nature First (2011). CreateSpace Publ./Amazon.com
Not Fit for a Dog: The Truth About Manufactured Dog and Cat Foods (2008), co-authored with Drs. Elizabeth Hodgkins and Marion E. Smart. Quill Driver Books, Sanger, CA.
Dog Body, Dog Mind: Exploring Your Dog's Consciousness and Total Well-Being (2007). The Lyons Press, Guilford, CT.
Cat Body, Cat Mind: Exploring Your Cat's Consciousness and Total Well-Being (2007). The Lyons Press, Guilford, CT.
Killer Foods: What Scientists Do to Make Genes Better is Not Always Best (2004). The Lyons Press, Guilford, CT.
The Healing Touch for Dogs (2004). New Market Press, NY.
The Healing Touch for Cats (2004). New Market Press, NY.
Bringing Life to Ethics: Global Bioethics for a Humane Society (2000). State University of New York Press, Albany, NY.
Beyond Evolution: The Genetically Altered Future of Plants, Animals, The Earth—And Humanity. (1999). The Lyons Press, Guilford, CT.

Eating With Conscience: The Bioethics of Food (1997). New Sage Press, Troutdale, OR.
The Boundless Circle (1996). Quest Books, Wheaton, IL.
Agricide: The Hidden Farm and Food Crisis That Affects Us All (Second edition 1996 of 1986 edition published by Schoken Books, NY). Krieger Publishing Co., Melbourne, FL.
Super Pigs and Wondercorn: The Brave New World of Biotechnology and Where It All Might Lead (1992). The Lyons Press, Guilford, CT. Subsequent revised editions: *Beyond Evolution: The Genetically Altered Future of Plants, Animals, The Earth...and Humans* (1999), and *Killer Foods: When Scientists Manipulate Genes, Better is Not Always Best* (2004).
The Soul of the Wolf (reprint edition 1992 of 1980 edition) Little, Brown, and Co. Boston MA) Lyons & Burford, NY.
Understanding Your Dog (revised edition 1992 of 1974 edition). Coward McCann and Geoghegan, Bantam Books, NY.), and Martin's Press, NY.
Understanding Your Cat (revised edition 1992 of 1974 edition published by Coward McCann and Geoghegan, NY then by Bantam Books NY.) St. Martin's Press, NY.
You Can Save the Animals: 50 Things You Can Do Right Now (1991). St. Martin's Press, NY.
Supercat: Raising the Perfect Feline Companion (1991). Howell Book House, NY.
Superdog: Raising the Perfect Canine Companion (1990). Howell Book House, NY.
Inhumane Society: The American Way of Exploiting Animals (1990). St. Martin's Press, NY.
The New Eden (1989). Lotus Press, Santa Fe, NM.
The New Animal Doctor's Answer Book (1989). Newmarket Press, NY.
Laboratory Animal Husbandry (1986). State University of New York Press, Albany, NY.
Between Animal and Man: The Key to the Kingdom (reprint edition 1986 of 1976 edition published by Coward, McCann and Geoghegan, NY). Krieger Publishing Co., Melbourne, FL.
The Whistling Hunters (1984). State University of New York Press, Albany, NY.
Behavior of Wolves, Dogs, and Related Canids (reprint edition 1984 of 1971 edition published by Jonathan Cape, London England). Krieger Publishing Co., Melbourne, FL.
The Dog: It's Domestication and Behavior (reprint edition 1987 of 1978 edition published by Garland STPM Press, NY). Krieger Publishing Co., Melbourne, FL.
One Earth, One Mind (reprint edition 1984 of 1980 edition published by Coward McCann and Geoghegan, NY). Krieger Publishing Co., Melbourne, FL.
Farm Animals: Husbandry, Behavior and Veterinary Practice: A Critic's Viewpoint (1984). University Press, Baltimore, MD.
The Healing Touch (1983). Newmarket Press, NY (paperback version of *Dr. Michael Fox's Massage Program for Cats and Dogs* (1981). Newmarket Press, NY. Subsequent editions: *The Healing Touch for Dogs* (2004) and *The Healing Touch for Cats* (2004).
Love is a Happy Cat (1982). Newmarket Press, New York.

How To Be Your Pet's Best Friend (1981). Coward, McCann & Geoghegan, New York.
Returning to Eden: Animal Rights and Human Responsibility (1980). Viking Press, New York.
Understanding Your Pet (1978). Coward, McCann and Geoghegan, New York.
Concepts in Ethology, Animal and Human Behavior (1974). University of Minnesota Press, Minneapolis MN. (second edition 1998). Krieger Publishing Co., Melbourne, FL.
Integrative Development of Brain and Behavior in the Dog (1971). University of Chicago Press, Chicago, IL.
Canine Pediatrics (1966). Charles C. Thomas Publishing, Springfield, IL.
Canine Behavior (1965). Charles C. Thomas Publishing, Springfield, IL.

Editor of:
Advances in Animal Welfare Science 1984, 1984/85 and 1986/87 with L.D. Mickley. Martinus Nijhoff Boston/Dordrecht.
The Wild Canids (reprint edition 1983 of 1975 edition published by Van Nostrand Reinhold Co. NY.). Krieger Publishing Co., Melbourne, FL.
On The Fifth Day: Animal Rights and Human Ethics (1977). Acropolis Press, Washington, DC (with R.K. Morris).
Readings in Ethology and Comparative Psychology (1973). Brooks/Cole, CA.
Abnormal Behavior in Animals (1968). W. B. Saunders, Philadelphia, PA.
Contributing Editor, *Encyclopedia Britannica*, 1996 edition, *Cat* and *Dog* entries.
Contributing Editor, *McCall's* Magazine, *Pet Life* column, 1974-1996.

Children's Books:
Animals Have Rights Too (1991). Crossroads/Continuum, NY.
The Way of the Dolphin (1981). Acropolis Books, Washington, DC.
The Touchlings (1981). Acropolis Books, Washington, DC.
Lessons From Nature: Fox's Fables (1980). Acropolis, Washington, DC.
Whitepaws: A Coyote-Dog (1979). Coward, McCann & Geoghegan, NY.
Wild Dogs Three (1977). Coward, McCann & Geoghegan, NY.
What Is Your Dog Saying? (1977). M. W. Fox and Wende Devlin Gates, Coward, McCann and Geoghegan, NY.
What Is Your Cat Saying? (1977). M. W. Fox and Wende Devlin Gates, Coward, McCann and Geoghegan, NY.
Ramu and Chennai * (1975). Coward, McCann & Geoghegan, NY.
Sundance Coyote ** (1974). Coward, McCann & Geoghegan, NY.
The Wolf *** (1973) Coward, McCann & Geoghegan, NY.
Vixie, The Story of a Little Fox (1973). Coward, McCann & Geoghegan, NY.
* Best Science Book Award, National Teachers' Association
** Nominee for Mark Twain Awards
*** Christopher Award for Children

In memory of Deanna L. Krantz and all we embraced.

Michael W. Fox

FOR ALL OUR RELATIONS

Poetic Visions and Vexations
of a Veterinarian

AUSTIN MACAULEY PUBLISHERS®
LONDON * CAMBRIDGE * NEW YORK * SHARJAH

Copyright © Michael W. Fox 2025

All rights reserved. No part of this publication may be reproduced, distributed, or transmitted in any form or by any means, including photocopying, recording, or other electronic or mechanical methods, without the prior written permission of the publisher, except in the case of brief quotations embodied in critical reviews and certain other non-commercial uses permitted by copyright law. For permission requests, write to the publisher.

Any person who commits any unauthorized act in relation to this publication may be liable to criminal prosecution and civil claims for damages.

Ordering Information
Quantity sales: Special discounts are available on quantity purchases by corporations, associations, and others. For details, contact the publisher at the address below.

Publisher's Cataloging-in-Publication data
Fox, Michael W.
For All Our Relations

ISBN 9798895433829 (Paperback)
ISBN 9798895433836 (ePub e-book)

Library of Congress Control Number: 2025900535

www.austinmacauley.com/us

First Published 2025
Austin Macauley Publishers LLC
40 Wall Street, 33rd Floor, Suite 3302
New York, NY 10005
USA

mail-usa@austinmacauley.com
+1 (646) 5125767

Michael W. Fox is eternally grateful for the spiritual and practical support of his wife Deanna Krantz and the gifts from all the animals, wild and domesticated, who came into our lives, and for our shared experiences caring for them and our communion with all the blessings of the natural world. Thanks also to Austin Macauley Publishers, for enabling me to share these experiences and relationships in this book.

Table of Contents

Message from the Dalai Lama	15
Introduction by Fr. Thomas Nathan Berry	16
Preamble	19
The Elegies	21
I Kurumbas, Elephants, and Jungle Shared	23
II Initiation and Renunciation	26
III Animal Slaughter	29
IV God Questions	31
V Nature Answers	35
VI Touching the Mirror: Entering All	37
VII Choosing Heaven or Hell	43
VIII Elephants: Broken Spirits, Breaking Hearts	47
IX When All Things Fall Apart, Gather Shadows, Face the Light	50
X The Outsiders from Nemesis to Apotheosis	53
The 'Empathosphere' and Compassion's Light	57
Collected Poems 1975–2024	65
I If Fish Could Scream	67
II The Panther	68
III Bovine Ruminations	70
IV They Came Down from the Trees	71
V I Knew a Child	72
VI God Right, God Wrong	73
VII New Year Reflections	74
VIII Coming to Sioux Falls, S. Dakota	75
IX August Evening	76
X Flying Not Away	77
XI Healing the Rain	78
XII The Beast Within	79
XIII In Wildness	80

XIII Becoming	81
XIV A Prayer for My Species	82
XV An Ode to Christmas Trees	84
XVI Going Fishing	85
XVII The Green People	86
XVIII For the Love of Wolves	87
XIX Advice to Brother Wolf	89
XX Thee Kill	90
XXI Hunters of the North	91
XXII For Ma'iingan (Ojibwe): Brother Wolf	92
XXIII Lamentation of the Larks	93
XXIII Man Eating Dog	94
XXIV Dogs to Me	95
XXV My Dog Batman	96
XXVI Sacred Elephants	98
XXVII Consuming Innocence and Animals	99
XXVIII What We Care to Eat	100
XXIX For Deanna—An Ode to Stones	102
XXX The Way of Reverence	103
XXXI Nature's Hidden Truths	104
XXXII For William Blake	106
XXXIII The Falling Towers	107
XXXIV The Way to Peace	110
XXXV Every Healer Knows	111
XXXVI Forever Healed	112
XXXVII The Holarchy	113
XXXVIII The End of the Race	115
XXXIV Evolve or Perish: A Paradigm Shift	116
XXXV One Pilgrim's Way	117
XXXVI For My Mother: In Memoriam	119
XXXVII Our Animal Relations	120
XXXVIII Help the Children	121

XXXIX For My Children	*122*
XL That God Be Damned!	*123*
XLI Trees of Life and Wisdom	*124*
XLII For Deanna: On Our Wedding Day	*125*
XLIII The Delta Sphynx	*126*
XLIV For Deanna: In Memoriam	*127*
XLV When I Write and Why	*128*

Message from the Dalai Lama

"Today, together with a growing appreciation of the importance of human rights, there is a greater awareness worldwide of the need for the protection not only of the environment, but also of animals and their rights. Unfortunately, there continue to be those who feel it is acceptable to hunt, abuse or exploit animals, resulting in their suffering and their painful deaths. This seems to contradict the general spirit of egalitarianism growing in most societies today.

I deeply believe that human beings are basically gentle by nature and I feel that not only should we maintain gentle and peaceful relations with our fellow human beings but that it is also very important to extend the same kind of attitude toward the environment and the animals who naturally live in harmony with it.

As a boy studying Buddhism in Tibet, I was taught the importance of a caring attitude toward others. Such a practice of nonviolence applies to all sentient beings—any living being that has a mind. Where there is a mind, there are feelings such as pain, pleasure and joy.

No sentient beings want pain; instead, all want happiness. Since we all share these feelings at some basic level, we, as rational human beings, have an obligation to contribute in whatever way we can to the happiness of other species and try our best to relieve their fears and sufferings.

The *Nilgiri Elegies: Reflections from the Indian Jungle on People, Animals and Nature* contains the poetic reflections of its author, Dr. Michael W. Fox, who, with his wife, Deanna Krantz, has been instrumental in establishing a refuge for animals in the Nilgiri Hills of South India.

It is a place where animals who have worked all their lives can retire, where sick animals can be healed. This work is an inspiring example of compassion in action. I firmly believe that the more we care for the happiness of others, the greater our own sense of well-being becomes.

Cultivating a close, warm-hearted feeling for others automatically puts the mind at ease. This helps remove our fears or insecurities and gives us the strength to cope with any obstacles we encounter. It is the ultimate source of success in life.

I pray not only that the help being given to animals in the Nilgiris may continue, but also that other people may be inspired to emulate this good work of setting up similar animal refuges elsewhere in the world."

The Dalai Lama
Dharamsala, India

Introduction by Fr. Thomas Nathan Berry

To mourn the pain and loss that we experience in the suffering and even the death of those dear to us is among the most profound and most admirable manifestations of our human mode of being. So too an insensitivity to the pain of others, the incapacity to experience sorrow indicates a diminished capacity to respond in any truly human manner to the realities of life.

All this is quite evident when the pain or loss is in the human world. The great challenge to our humanity is the extent to which our emotional response reaches beyond the human into the larger world of living beings, into the world of those who, like us, possess consciousness and a feeling soul.

To be alive is by definition to possess a soul, to be an ensouled being. Indeed, a soul is defined as the primary sustaining and activating form of a living organic being. As all expressions of nature are differentiated, so too with living beings.

So, in nature, there are plants along with human and non-human animals. All of us in the living world are bonded together in a mutual relationship. We cannot survive without each other.

Our affection for the animals, our concern for their well-being, our ability to celebrate with them the wonder of existence, to mourn their pain and grieve over their death is a measure of the human quality of our lives. They do no less for us. Our dogs, particularly, express their grief when we are in pain.

They suffer with us, they shield us from harm with their own lives, they understand and mourn our death. Thomas Aquinas, the medieval theologian, says, in one of his commentaries on Dionysus, that the entire created world is bound together in a 'bond of friendship'.

The tragedy of the present is not simply what we are doing to the entire living world of our times, it is what we are doing to ourselves. We can only note with a touch of dismay the manner in which we read the accounts of the extinctions, not merely of individuals, but of entire species, that we are causing throughout the planet.

We read the accounts and then go about our daily routine as unconcerned as if we had simply noted that it was a cloudy day. We seem not to realize the extent to which we are limiting our capacity for compassion and for mourning the loss of some of our dearest earth companions.

That the scale of suffering and death that we are inflicting on these vulnerable members of our living community is so monumental, makes the comprehension and the compassion immensely more significant.

Such has been the mission of Michael W. Fox for the past forty years. He has written over forty books on the role of animals and the care they need from us. As a veterinarian with immense compassion, he has also cared for innumerable individual animals.

Together with his wife, Deanna Krantz, he has established an animal refuge for animals in India, a country where humans and animals are dependent on each other, but where the human care, as in most of the world, is often completely missing.

Here, he has gone beyond any work to write a series of elegies, elegies like no other elegies that I have ever read. Here, we mourn the afflictions that we, as humans, are inflicting on the animals in the wild and in their domestic setting.

He is especially aware of the torment imposed on wild elephants to make them docile and obedient to human commands. As no one in recent times, he has mourned the fate of animals in a period when humans have become ruthless in their determination to make every earthly being serve the human masters of the planet on which we live.

Yet Michael W. Fox, throughout the work, has the gift of mitigating the sorrow he expresses with a remarkable sense of an emerging empathosphere, an all-enfolding pathos capable of ennobling the human while it brings a healing presence to all living creatures.

It has been said that compassion is the quintessence of religion. In its expressed ideals, Buddhism, among the classical religious traditions, has expressed a unique concern for the suffering of other living beings.

Santi Deva, in the 5th century of our era, made a vow to take upon himself the suffering of all living beings, considering that "it was better that he alone should suffer than that so many others should live in torment."

While there have been notable instances of compassion for animals in our western tradition, persons such as Saint Francis of Assisi, who spoke of animals as our brother creatures, the more general attitude is that any emphasis on animals having souls would detract from the unique quality of the human soul.

Even more than this, however, is the denial of any living principle in the animal world by the western scientific tradition since the early 17th century when René Descartes taught that animals were mechanisms.

The real failure of understanding in our own western world is the failure to appreciate the extent to which we are dependent on our experience of the natural world around us for our own human and spiritual development. We fail to realize that without our experience of the outer world of nature, we would have no interior spiritual insight or appreciation.

If we lived on the moon, our minds and imagination would be limited by the impressions we would receive from the barren landscape. The absence of any living being such as we experience here on earth would make our interior life of mind and soul impossible.

In more recent times, a greater sense of the animal soul has come into being, a recognition of the knowing and feeling capacities of these companion beings that share life with us here on the planet Earth. If the ability to manifest compassion is a measure, then our domestic animals, especially our dogs, have a quality in their presence and their affection that, in many cases, reaches beyond what humans are able to provide.

What humans need is a sympathetic appreciation and dedicated concern not merely of those animals that live with us but even more for that vast number of wilderness animals that reveal to us the full wonder of existence in their form and movement and voice.

We need to reflect not simply on the benefits of our industrial society but even more on the cruelty it is inflicting on the living world about us. If we have benefited from its assistance, we have lost immeasurably from its death-dealing consequences throughout the world of the living.

I can hardly say enough in praise of this work that Michael W. Fox has given us, both for its content and for the manner of its presentation. If we would ponder what he is saying, we would understand our historical situation and our own personal lives more fully.

Riverdale Center for Religious Research
New York, NY

Preamble

After working as a veterinarian and animal protection advocate for 40 years, I returned to the Nilgiri or Blue Mountains in Tamil Nadu, South India, in 1995. (The Tamil word *Nilgiri* translates into Blue Mountains). I had been invited to give the opening address at the Indian Veterinary Association's annual conference in Hissar, North India.

My wife, Deanna Krantz, accompanied me, and before the veterinary conference, we first visited the Nilgiris where I had done field studies of the pack-hunting Asiatic wild dog or dhole some twenty years earlier.

This region is one of the wildest places left on the Indian sub-continent and was recently designated by the United Nations as a Global Biosphere Reserve—a world treasure of cultural and biological diversity. For me, it felt like my original (aboriginal) home, awakening all my senses including the sense of the sacred.

We had no preconception that our lives would be changed forever and that one year later, we would return to the Nilgiris where Deanna would start the India Project for Animals and Nature (IPAN) to help improve the health and welfare of thousands of domestic animals, provide free veterinary services and dog spay/neuter in poor villages and tribal communities; establishing a refuge for hundreds of animals from dogs to donkeys and monkeys to water buffalo, and help save the last of the wild.

Nor did we anticipate the physical hardships and emotional and financial challenges of living on two continents, often for months apart. As we put together India's finest animal refuge at Hill View Farm, we faced local opposition from various corrupt authorities and vested interest groups, and documented some of the most horrendous animal cruelty imaginable.

This was in stark contrast to the beauty of the place that I sought to capture in IPAN's first newsletter as follows:

Around Hill View Farm Animal Refuge

Emerging from the night through the mist and low clouds, the Blue Mountains move from indigo and purple as the first peacock cries as dawn breaks and a troop of langur monkeys whoop and bark at the panther slouching home beneath them into the invisibility of cool shadows where the wild boars root, cobras and hyenas awaken to the sun while a family of elephants walk down sunbeams to the river to drink and bathe beside a herd of dappled deer.

The otters are playing upstream from a spotted deer's remains that the wild dogs have just left to the flies, a shy jackal and two hungry dogs from the waking village for where smoke is rising as people boil their water and rice, clanging milk churns and calling their cows, a timeless mantra echoing in the rustling stands of bamboo.

Along the river, a shimmer of dragonflies, the babble of water and stones becomes the babble of warblers and orioles in the deep jungle, breathing with the seasons, for eons dreaming into life the infinite, the mystery, the beauty, and the silence between the pulse of last night's sacred drums as tribals danced into the night in the refuge's donkey corral, and two of some thirty rescued dogs toasted themselves beside the fire.

The elegies that follow are drawn from some of my experiences while working at Deanna's refuge in the Nilgiris, and from the inspiration and reflection on a lifetime working for animals that was enhanced by being with this woman and in this unforgettable place that the rest of the world knows so little about.

Much of what I want to express and share is in the ethos or spirit of the narrative elegy. This is because of the graphic, almost mythic imagery I experience while contemplating what I have learned in the company of animals, and what I have witnessed in how animals are regarded and treated around the world.

Furthermore, I believe that the poetic format of these elegies provides a more concise, if not more penetrating, review and understanding of the nature of animals and of our humanity and inhumanity, than would a more impersonal, scientifically documented, and footnoted report in the usual prose format.

I have done much of that kind of documentation elsewhere (see *India's Animals: Helping the Sacred and the Suffering* by Deanna L. Krantz and Michael W. Fox. Create Space books, 2016). The poetic realm I regard as that realm of human perception and insight that is more immediate, heart-centered, empathic, and subjective than the realm of objective, scientific rationalism.

Cruelty to animals, suffering, the extinction of species and indigenous peoples, and the end of the wild, are concerns that cannot be resolved by reason and scientific objectivity alone. Empathy, subjectivity, and imagination are also called for since they are integral to the formulation and practice of ethics and spirituality as I often discussed with my dear friend 'Geologian' Thomas Berry.

I am as leery of the term spirituality as of the catch phrase 'science-based' or 'scientifically determined', because of the harms caused by fundamentalist believers in the 'truths' of scientific and religious dogma as being absolute and exclusive, rather than potentially complementary and mutually enhancing.

Traditionally, science deals with the material and the objectively quantifiable, while spirituality addressing the non-material, the universal and subjective realms of human experience. One role of poetry is to bring these two world views together in real time and space; what I see as a 'grounding' of the life of the mind in quantum field entanglements of biological realism with its metaphysical and bioethical ramifications.

Such grounding opens us up to the realm of the sensuous, and to the divine mystery of eternal presence, or 'beingness', the realm of the sacred. After the elegies, I have included an essay that relates to my experiences with the animals at our refuge that I regard as the gifts of compassionate action from creatures great and small.

The Elegies

I
Kurumbas, Elephants, and Jungle Shared

To whom can I speak of this place
of wild beauty now ravaged, defiled?
Where once the jungle trembled with life,
the king bull elephants are all gone,
almost the tiger, panther and bear,
along with all the great trees,
rosewood, banyan, sandalwood, teak,
and the perennial Moyar and Sigur rivers
now poisoned and seasonally dry.
To whom shall I cry where compassion,
conservation and concern are all a lie?
Where life is so cheap and tribals who care
dare not speak as they wait for the end.
I shall bear witness and speak for them.
Or am I too late and all effort in vain
to save the spirit and life of this place
that in earlier years I hallowed as home?
Will I soon be turning in my grave
beneath a silent heaven, a muted world,
where once I witnessed the miracles
of one woman's love, courage, healing powers;
and the compassionate action she inspired.
The Kurumba tribal people named her
after their jungle deity 'Mariamma'
fierce protector of the innocent, healer of the incurable
and whom I knew as my wife, Deanna.
For several years, she and her devoted local staff
ran an animal refuge nestled in the Nilgiris,
the Blue Mountains of the Western Ghats
in southern India, giving tender care
to the animals of the poor in surrounding villages
and tribal communities.
The Kurumbas taught me that there can be dignity
where there is poverty.
But where there is poverty of spirit,
there is no hope. We gave them hope,
when they saw our work that won their trust,
becoming a voice for their rights
and all that they held sacred in the jungle, their home.
They became our informants when elephants, bison
and other wild creatures were killed,
streams diverted, wild fruit trees felled

illegally by rich land owners;
and brought wild orphans for us to heal and release.
I have written these elegies for the animals,
and for our Kurumba tribal friends
who, while trekking through the jungle
as fast as I can keep up, see
an elephant footprint on the trail
and within an instant know which one,
how recent, and what direction
so not to be killed by walking on without regard
as they continue a quietly animated conversation
while they laugh and glide on wide bare feet.
These people, long respected in the Nilgiris
for their powers of sorcery and divination,
as well as knowledge of medicinal plants,
and the ways of elephants and jungle life,
know that only that which is sacred is secure.

There are different Kurumba groups,
like the Hill, Elephant, and Honey Kurumbas,
each specialized in particular ways,
either farming in the hills,
working with captive elephants,
or gathering honey and other forest produce
that sustained a subsistence way of life
for countless generations.
This was only possible because
they are good accountants,
taking no more from the forest
than the forest community can afford to share.
They live within nature's economy,
the essence of wisdom's ethical boundaries
of enlightened self-restraint.
Outsiders call this primitivism they link
with poverty in their ignorance
of the matrix, the web of life
wherein there is no hierarchy,
only radiance, symmetry, and more peace
than chaos, suffering, and despair.

As animists, Kurumbas see the spirit within all;
all creatures, and every living and non-living being.
But they are threatened now
by all that is destroying their jungle home,
their culture, religion, dreams,
security and identity.
The killing of one more elephant,
illegal felling of one more tree,

and the birth of one more goat or child
outside the tribe, the jungle,
in the quickening chaos beyond,
they see approaching like a forest fire.

They now know all about Monsanto
since I told their leaders and elders
and village farmers of the region
at a community gathering to Save the Nilgiris
through good farming practices
and traditional 'social' forestry.
After my talk, one tribal elder
shaking his head at the dirt floor
with eyes half closed, remembering, said,
"These big corporations come now,
like the British before them,
full of great promises.
They took out our greatest trees
to make floors and doors,
shot all the wild animals for trophies,
and turned us into coolies
for their railroads and plantations."
These aboriginal, original First People
respect the web of life,
the sacred womb of Earth inseparable
from their religion, politics and economy.
The 'cultured' man would rather sleep
on a mattress than like a Kurumba on a dirt floor mat.
So, cultured man turns the odd louse and bed bug,
who thrive in mattresses, into an infestation.
The more civilized Kurumbas have no need for pesticides,
and could never seek to profit
from their own mistakes and at others' expense.
These people are connected with the jungle
and all that sustains them
because in mind and body
they are joined with the spirit
of all that lives and breathes,
from trees to rivers, rocks to dreams.
Life in a rock is life that sleeps.
Life in a plant is life that feels.
Life in an animal is life that knows.
The 'civilized' man is unaware
of sacred connections, not seeing the web,
because he never sees the cow
who gives him milk, or her calf, his flesh,
and supple, long-lasting skin to wear,
to make shoes to walk unfeeling on the Earth.

II
Initiation and Renunciation

Observing, tracking, and researching
the dhole, Asiatic wild dog of the Nilgiris
some forty years ago,
now another endangered species,
I learned to feel in the wind's direction,
and the cadence of bamboo,
if it was safe to proceed
and not be killed by an elephant.
The Kurumbas once could walk among them,
maintaining their respectful distance
of humility and awe, and were never killed.
I have walked over elephant tracks
with the Kurumbas whose sorcery
is in their power to see the web,
since we are all like spiders,
but live in invisible cocoons and webs.
We make the invisible visible,
like Rilke's 'bees of the invisible',
when sense becomes feeling
and feeling is seeing.
Then we are clear.
So is their way, and without fear.
But being fearless will not suffice,
for there are forces worse
than any jungle-spirit might materialize,
that are destroying the web forever,
and turning elephants into ivory
and into killers and slaves.
Forever and all for why?
By what decree, or force of circumstance,
that some call progress,
and others call the End of Days
should the world stand by
and let this happen?
The death of nature, and the web
of all our sacred connections and relations.

The Kurumba animists see all.
They look into the fire
as they dance and sing around it,
knowing that human life
is also a flame, flickering,

but of a different kind:
A flame that asks how and why,
and all to what end,
as the jungle night informs it,
and still inspires to light
the greater darkness of the human soul.

Before they were colonized,
some would say civilized,
by the European state of mind,
aboriginal people lived well
according to a spirituality
that equated survival and prosperity
with simplicity and obedience to nature.

Australian aboriginal Bill Neidjie said,
"If you feel soreheadache, sore body,
that mean somebody killing tree or grass.
You feel because your body in that tree or earth
No body can tell you,
You got to feel it yourself."
But who feels anymore?
The First People took no more from the land
than would sustain their basic needs,
and never more. But for the colonizers,
more was not enough: All or nothing
was the creed of greed and progress,
of military and bureaucratic imperialism
and religious missionary zeal of mammonism.
All to what end, but the loss of humanity,
of cultural and natural diversity.
The sanctity and integrity of the original people
and their relationships with the natural world
hold no meaning or value to the modern mind
except as a resource to exploit and sell,
or as obstacles to suppress, exterminate,
or assimilate.

To call into question this dominant worldview
is to be called a neo-Luddite,
anti-science, anti-progress.

After generations of living
like wild animals in zoos, bereft of dignity,
separated from their roots and customs,
so much traditional wisdom lost,
the choices of assimilation or extinction
and the weight of alcohol and suicide

challenge the last of our living ancestors:
The tribal gatherer-hunters, the pastoralists,
and once community sustaining farmers and fishermen.
Those who cry, "Earth First!" Not people and commerce,
see human and animal liberation as one;
as one movement for the liberation of life
from the tyranny of human arrogance,
ignorance, indifference and greed.
The war against inhumanity
and the depravity of our kind
goes on regardless of the outcome
for fight we must for justice and compassion.
In these dark and sickening times,
the affluent, who could do so much,
live in denial of others' quiet desperation,
despair and suffering, as the End Time draws near.

III
Animal Slaughter

We followed them, Deanna, and I,
to slaughter. The sheep, the goats,
the fattened water buffalo calves,
bewildered, driven hard, too tired to cry.
We saw the sacred cows tied in bunches
with ropes, through bleeding noses,
as they plodded, stumbled, pulled
each other down; crippled cows,
spent cows; dry and sterile cows;
collapsing cows, exhausted from the march.
Hooves worn down to bloody pulp.
Tails twisted, broken, hammered
to get them up; others weeping
from the salt and chili pepper in their eyes
rubbed in to get them up and moving; others tied
and piled in flat-bed trucks,
dying, stifling, stiffening and dead.
Then came the water buffaloes
who like the cows were kept for milk
and were once treated like family.
Their eyes were filled with terror,
disbelief; the ultimate betrayal.
So too the eyes of worn-out bullocks,
many, walking skeletons of hide and bones,
who once pulled carts and ploughs.
When young, they had their testicles pulverized
between two flat rocks or teakwood blocks.
I remembered touching one trembling bullock,
eyes rolled back in semi-conscious shock
soon after this barbaric operation
I was too late to stop.
Then came the calves, tied in bunches,
unwanted bull calves, half-starved
for lack of mother's milk,
weak with parasites and insides
filled with knotted masses
of plastic bags from the garbage
in the streets, the only food for most.
In the slaughterhouse, my nostrils burned
with the mingled stench of fear,
blood and sweat in a spinning world
where slaughter men put out the light

in eyes of cow and buffalo, lamb and goat,
and fixed the frozen gaze of death.
The little goats had cried like children,
"maa-maa-ma," for their mothers.
I saw them dragged in bunches
to the killing slab and flashing knives.
I saw the world of beast and man falling apart
with no ritual slaughter or any reverence,
as throats were hacked, not swiftly sliced,
while animals waited, trembling and seeing all.

That night, the flying shards of shattered souls
that filled the air with broken light,
all came together in my dream
as one heaving, steaming, bloody mass,
of writhing, screaming spirals
of bone, nerve, tendon, and raw flesh.
This archetypal beast of suffering,
while being skinned alive and drawn and quartered,
twisted around with one eye left
to focus, piercing my heart with pain.
Returning from the festival of the temple
of Massi Karibuntan Aya in the Nilgiri forest,
our Kurumba animal refuge staff,
whose hearts were opened by their work,
were shaking as they recounted all that they had seen:
One hundred and fifty garlanded, bleating goats in line
waiting to be decapitated on the temple steps.
Children watched and their relatives waited
around the lips of a slow cascade of blood,
to receive the bodies for the public feast.
The heads were taken by the priest for temple staff.
White rice donated by the local rich
bubbled and steamed for thousands of waiting mouths.
Many goats in waiting cried in terror.
What child heart was not also touched,
but turned to stone by end of day?
Who entered the silence after the bleat cut short
and saw the emptiness in dead goats' eyes
mirroring the crowd's?
All light and spirit gone
in sacrifice to what?

IV
God Questions

In India, digging maggots from the wounds
of cows and dogs who were being eaten alive,
I wondered, above the stench and suffering,
if there was a god.
I saw temple icons of gods in animal form;
the elephant god, Ganesh,
Nandi, the sacred bull,
and Hanuman, the monkey god.
The people bowed and prayed before them,
placing offerings of flowers and food to secure
divine concessions,
while outside everywhere, real animals suffered
more than the poorest of the poor
sick, injured, starving and afraid;
others chained or whipped,
goaded and overloaded.
The sacred and the suffering were one.

In America, investigating livestock factories
where calves, pigs and poultry were so crowded
in pens and stalls, they could never run or feel the sun;
and animal research laboratories, so clean and sterile,
where tree-swinging monkeys
and love-lost dogs were caged for life
I wondered if there was a god.
I discovered other gods:
The gods of progress, profit and productivity,
of scientific knowledge and Aesculapian authority.
Regardless then of culture and belief
for the animals, there is no relief, no redress:
And surely no redemption East or West
for those whose gods
serve human ends alone.
While some feel awe and wonder
in the presence of other animal forms
and see God in all, and all in God,
others blame their god for the world's suffering
and see it as evidence of God's abandonment,
retribution, or as proof there is no god.
Then atheism, nihilism and fatalism flourish
in a world made mute and incoherent
by our separation from the whole.

What kind of god would make a world
where wild dogs tear and eat the fawn alive
and some men beat and blind elephants in chains?
What god could make a living world
of such miraculous beauty and diversity
that we find in wildness and wilderness,
from the play of light on peacock plumes,
to the different sounds
of dancing trees before the rains,
and yet allow so much harm and suffering?
Is the miraculous, like beauty, mere illusion?

Or are the dualities of love and hate,
cruelty and compassion, the antipodes
that we must navigate,
with the compass of compassion,
between order and chaos, harmony and despair?
Did God make us to help, to intercede,
to serve as empathic healers, co-creators
for a Creation, not flawed or fallen,
but not yet complete without our involvement,
in this world's evolvement?
The first act of Creation was separation
of the One Self into otherness,
the Universal becoming the particular:
Non-being into being;
the Absolute into the relative;
the Immortal into the mortal
and the Eternal into the temporal.
From the primal unity of the plenum-void
came multiplicity and diversity.
Life giving life, taking life
one life by and for another.
Duality and reality are one.
Where there is separation, there is duality.
Without separation, there is no individuation,
no freedom, fulfillment, or suffering and death.

By what divine conception
or evolutionary progression
have most humans been empowered
with the choice between good and evil,
and have a conscience to know the difference?
By what divine conception
or developmental progression
have most humans and other animals
been given the gift of empathy,
to feel the suffering of others?

In our minds, the shadows
of doubt, fear and delusion
create a void of confusion,
so, we separate self from other,
being from non-being,
the dream from reality,
feeling from action,
and dreaming from becoming.
Other animals on their certain paths,
with pure sight and light of innocence,
devoid of self-doubt, move along
a different path and show the way.
When we suffer them to come to us
with loving kindness and respect,
we will not regain our innocence,
but will be open to the world again,
and reclaim the ancient way.
In their eyes, we will see reflected
our own humanity.
The deeper nature of silent beasts
tangible through their presence and essence
lies beyond our full embrace and understanding.
Burning like a fire in the wild distance
of a history more remote than ours,
yet born from the same stardust and light
they took a different path than we,
without question or any doubt,
born with a certainty beyond faith and hope.

What of those whose path we change
becoming captives of heart or cage;
creating dependence, demanding obedience,
betraying their truth by turning their path
to serve our own ends, selfish and profane?
Do they then, like us, question? Doubt?
needing faith and hope to endure as we,
the great loneliness and longing;
the separation of nature from spirit,
and self from all?
What can free them can make us whole.
I once thought that compassion
is our greatest power on Earth.
But I have learned in the darkest hours
of witnessing cruelty and others' suffering,
and being unable to intercede,
that surrender and supplication
to the Higher Power is a vital invocation
to focus our greatest power, compassion,

as during prayer, contemplation,
and preparation for war,
in the right direction for right action.
The outward prayer is for others,
including those who cause suffering
for empathy is selflessness.
The inner prayer involves the war
between freedom and responsibility;
helplessness and outrage;
and selfish indifference and loving kindness.
Through the powers of love and self-control
and belief in freedom for all,
we become the truth we live by,
embracing silence
and the stillness of nesting cranes.

V
Nature Answers

Nature shares her secrets when our hearts are open
and we are mindful of our relationships,
respectful of all our ancestors and relations,
human and non-human; animal and plant.
Every living being has her place and role
within the sacred, boundless circle
whose center is everywhere.
All are free to be themselves,
obedient to their Creator
by being true to their nature
within the boundaries of Natural Law,
that stem from universal principles
a more enlightened humanity
would conscientiously embrace.
For most other animals, these principles
are part inborn, and part imposed without
like self-restraint and mutual care.

All beings through their place and role
within the seamless web of earthly life,
thus co-evolve and co-create.
So might we, with open hearts,
and being mindful of the Law,
define and refine ourselves universally
by virtue, justice, harmony and peace.

Will humility and self-restraint
mean freedom for all?
If to care for one is to care for all
members of the Earth community,
will we not find harmony, justice, and peace
illumed by a democracy of spirit,
united by the right and will to be?
Other creatures, belonging to the wheel of life,
maintain, sustain, renew the world,
their covenant unbroken, to their natures true:
The sun bear takes the honey
from the bees who pollinate the flowering forest
Kurumbas share with spotted deer and dancing hare.
Sprouting from elephants' sunbaked droppings
mushrooms of many hues send out their spores
that breezes and shaking fur spread for miles

into the forest to bring the dead to life
when spores germinate and weave their silver threads
of mycelia throughout the breathing soil,
digesting the inedible to feed the trees.
Through elephants and mushrooms,
life cycling through life in myriad associations,
the circle is complete,
and the forest is renewed.
Why then do humans tear the web apart
and make their own dysfunctional facsimile
with such blind, industrious devotion?
Is it some lethal biological aberration,
a mutation into a parasite
that infests and kills its host?
Or is this proclivity to harm and desecrate
some disease, a virus of the soul
we can control through empathy,
showing our children how the power of love
can heal, make whole the web of life
that love of power and ignorance destroy?

VI
Touching the Mirror: Entering All

Heart of the beast, true to herself,
radiates the beauty of divine nature's mystery.
Who sees and feels, knows there is only 'Thou'.
Other animals can teach us not to lie
and how indeed to die and live our truth.
Plant kingdom, turning stone to flesh and bone,
stardust into apples, sunlight into firelight.
Animal wisdom, inborn and acquired,
unifying form and spirit, Earth, and soul
forever bound in sacred presence
for our remembrance and embrace.
The mind of one in all;
the universal in the particular,
the particular in the universal.
One Earth. One Mind.
One Health. One Economy.
Mind in the waters, the forests, the skies.
Elephants in their jungle dreaming;
leopards breathing in dappled shade;
life giving to life, preserving the light.

The scent and taste of tamarind,
mushroom, melon, yam, awaken
the ancient wisdom of what is good
in the garden of earthly delights,
bringing to us pleasure and satisfaction.
How else could it be for other animals
whose senses, more acute than ours
attune and guide them to what is good
and right for them.
The vibrant colors of spring flowers;
a sound or movement in the grass;
a gentle touch by a trusted other;
the comfort of anointed lair and nest;
security of flock, shoal, swarm and herd.
In the realm of the senses, we and they
share so much—in feeling too
and so, in spirit and in deed.

Let me take you in your dreaming
into the deep scented sounds of jungle night
where your eyes will become the stars

and your feet feel the earth's living power
rise through you as you dance into the dawn
with forest spirits and tribal ancestors
mingling with the dancers, flute
and fire-tensed drums into the cool of morning.
Then you will find in the wild heart
of darkness, the animist powers
that make your love and life fearless and complete.

Looking at the ashes in the morning's rising
around the shrine of fire, we danced and laughed
and seared our souls in the goddess of the flames,
I see the footprints of our Kurumba friends
where they danced and sang to elephants,
in their jungle and to the stars above,
melding with those of donkeys and other animals
who now move quietly around me at
our animal refuge in the Nilgiri Hills
waiting to be tended and fed:
A peaceable kingdom whose circle of light
is an island of hope in an ocean of suffering.
When you look into the Light,
your eyes will water into stars,
and if you weep, you will feel
the salt in your tears returning
to the primal sea.
Within the Light, we all abide
in oceans of joy and promise,
as well as others' suffering and gratitude.
But for the dry eye and cold heart
there is neither Light nor hope,
no insight or vision free of the weight
of self and nothing else.
Then life eternal becomes an endless round
of desiring, consuming, exploiting, possessing:
The hell on Earth of eternal of chaos,
darkness, suffering and delusion.

Seeing animals in different ways
because of what we feel and want,
we treat some like family,
others as our slaves and property.
Some are pets, others pests.
Some ego-trophies, others eco-totems.

Some are sacrificed to gods and science,
others skinned or shorn and worn,
or fattened, killed, and cooked,

for reasons sanctified by custom,
and wants so rarely questioned.
What of the innocence of the lamb,
tied for slaughter?
What of the innocence of all creatures
whom we chain, and cage
despite all of heaven's rage?
What fallen kind could beat
elephants in chains to obey,
or shoot them for their tusks,
harpoon the great whales,
race horses to death,
put their genes into pigs
to make them organ donors
and give AIDS to chimpanzees
and syphilis, in the arrogant belief
that it is right because
the animals are sub-human?
What then does it mean to be human
and what makes us better than they?
Might makes right when the lover of power
usurps the power of love.

Seeing animals as reflections of our selves
with needs, interests, loves, fears, a life of their own,
could we still treat them as things inferior?
Only our denial of the nature of reality
leads us to regard other beings as of less significance
and sanctity than we,
unworthy of equal and fair regard.
Yet every creature is a Word of God
as every species is a nation unto itself.

What will the world become if we do not resist
the harmful forces of spiritual corruption
that many now, and future generations all
will call the norm and do nothing
but preserve the status quo of a depraved existence?
All that makes us human will then be extinct,
along with all that once was wild, natural.
The fight against the extinction of the tiger,
the elephant and other animal nations
is bound inexorably with the fight
against the extinction of the human spirit
and all that our better natures still embrace.
The human remains in the embryo
limbo of ego until the shell
of selfishness and delusion of separateness

is shattered so that when we enter
the forest, the forest enters us,
and we learn the language of the trees.
And then when animals speak to us
we will hear and understand with open hearts.
St. Francis of Assisi called this shattering
our 'second birth'. For our aboriginal ancestors,
this death and rebirth came through
the vision quest and rites of initiation.
Otherwise, we would remain an imitation
of the fully human, perpetually pubescent,
adolescent addled-essence poisoning
our souls and all we touch on Earth.

All animals reflecting the divine,
are a mirror to the human soul.
They reveal to us the God in all
and the good and bad in each of us
in how we see and treat them.
In their love and trust and fear and suffering,
they are kindred with angelic beings
who come to show us all the way.
But they and we, and all that is natural
will soon be gone unless we recognize
the sanctity of life as tangible
as the perfume of the morning rose
and the breath of golden dogs
in morning's Garden of Eternal Light.

At the Gathering of Shamans, I heard a song:
"Keep your face to the sunshine
and you will not see your shadow."
The path of these Elegies takes us
repeatedly into the darkest shadows
of human nature's imperfections,
that we for nature's sake can gather
on any rising path toward the light,
'for all paths that rise, converge'.
In our embrace of darkness, we find the Light.

Gathering out shadows, we may better understand
the nature of truth and the truth of nature,
for it is said that there is no higher religion
than truth. Then we face the sunshine
with open, heart-clear minds.
Honesty of heart and clarity of mind
were the virtues, values life skill legacies
of Shamanic and other Earth-centered traditions,

passed down from generation to generation
by healers, teachers, parents;
now almost lost to the cacophony of cyberspace,
to the selfish prattle of an all-consuming interspace,
and other virtual realities snared in the realm of *maya*,
of living in deluded absence of the sacred.
Like wood to fire, sanctioned cruelty and accepted suffering
ignite the flames of separation and indifference,
and then all humanity is lost.
Being thus separated and indifferent,
we should not be surprised
that we will continue to get sicker
and sicken the Earth with our chemicals
and poisoned and polluting ways; and in the process,
make other animals suffer ever more
to find cures for our stupidity.
We also seek more lethal means to kill each other,
when economic coercion and diplomacy fail,
and terrorists attack again.
What a silly way to live, making heaven into hell.
Before I entered my first sweat lodge,
I was told to pray for all my Earth relations
and that meant all the non-human ones,
not simply those of my own race.
We are all connected, genetically related,
same genes in our babies, bananas, and bees,
the gene engineers report,
still taken aback by finding
fewer genes in humans than in
the genome of a grain of rice.

I hope the next biology, like the new physics,
will help us correct the equation
of what it means to be human,
otherwise, the biotechnology industry
will have more harmful and enduring consequences
than the petrochemical engineering industry before them:
and require incredibly advanced and costly
new corrective biotechnologies in the future,
whatever that may hold,
if we cannot all keep our faces to the sunshine,
or hold another's gaze.

When we enter the spirit of the body
as the elders and shamans showed,
we know that the body is in the spirit.
We discover the colors of communion
in the powers of our natural senses

that the love and wisdom of nature can ignite,
to the open mind and the honest and brave of heart.
Our gift of life is a gift for all
in the life of Spirit, indwelling,
omnipresent, illimitable-the 'Power of the World',
as Sioux medicine man Black Elk
called the essence of life,
to help his people see with open hearts.
Not for themselves did they keep
their faces to the sunshine,
but for the good and grace of
brothers and sisters in the sun dance,
and all our relations beneath, above, and around.
Being able to enter the spirit of the body
our ancestors knew how to die,
as well as to live in dignity and with prescience
within the living spirit that unites us all
in a life of ever deepening communion,
suffering and joy, with the power to heal ourselves,
and to awaken both warrior and sage within.

VII
Choosing Heaven or Hell

Milton in *Paradise Lost* wrote,
"The mind is its own place and in itself
can make a Heaven of Hell, a Hell of Heaven."
The hell or heaven within our minds
is the hell or the heaven without.
Mind and world are one
in joy and tribulation, and in spirit and soul;
in time and history, in space and place.
How can anyone be surprised
by acts of rape,
of men violating women,
even little children,
in cultures that rape
the minds of little children,
and kill or murder innocence,
imagination and freedom of thought:
That rape the forests, mountains, rivers, seas,
destroying other cultures, and private lives,
in the name of freedom, the American way:
Or the way of other gods, be they
in graven images or waving flags
in subcontinents of malcontents.

When we see elephants in the wild,
we acknowledge that they are free.
Free to be, to come and go as they choose.
But what is freedom but a word
most abused by vested interests
who tout freedom as enterprise,
the right to make might right,
to put the ox or coolie before the cart,
to ride on top of elephants
and inside jumbo jets
for reasons of business, pleasure,
like playing golf on green and verdant courses
in the middle of a desert or once a wildlife preserve;
or going trophy-hunting in jungles and savannas.
What's good for animals and the environment
is good for people and the world economy.
So away with golf, obscene theme parks, tourism
and elephant rides, so we may have an economy
of less harm, and more sanity and sanctity for all.

We will only be moved to end
the holocaust of indigenous peoples and animals,
and the hell we make of Earth,
when our deepest instinct is awakened;
the survival instinct, that reason informs
means recreating a clean and healthful environment,
with pure food, water, air and rain.
This means a humane and compassionate society
with vision shared to heal the Light;
the atmosphere now disintegrating from our
collective thermal and chemical assault
that turns the sun's rays of life into the death rays
of nature's retribution-our nemesis.
Reason also informs that humankind
is an endangered species like the lion and elephant,
because all that makes us human
our humanity—will soon become extinct.
So, wherever we are, in the ghetto, stock exchange,
corporate board room, or refugee camp,
we must protect those values and virtues
that codify the survival instinct
into ethics, justice, and compassionate action
that lights the candles of loving kindness
by whose lights we can be guided and inspired.
When I found that there was no center left to hold
and all that I embraced and lived for was buried
under lies, disinformation and deception,
and by the charades of spirituality and official concern,
I ceased to be bound by success and failure.
All the norms of situational ethics
and the morality of civilized society
ceased to exist in the absence of the sacred.
I accepted what was, and turning inward
found the wisdom of hindsight affirming
the noble futility of good intentions
in a milieu of insatiable and profane self-interest
where conscience, compassion and rule of law
were as hard to find as cuckoos in their nests.
Suspicion, injustice and abuse of power
now stalk the world, poisoned,
malevolent and rent by cunning and discontent:
A hell on Earth for all to witness;
the tragic consequence of spiritual corruption
and of souls half rabid behind the masks
of civility, concern and saving face,
when all that makes us human is almost gone
and the End Time is upon each and everyone.

"If you come to India to do good work,
you must be stealthy," a local businessman advised.
I believed him because I saw how his dog,
whom he had brought to me for veterinary attention,
responded to him with a wag of his stumpy tail
when he spoke his name, and dogs don't lie.

Coming to India to do good, we were initially treated
with suspicion because no one trusts or can be trusted.
I was slow to learn to be stealthy
around the poor and the wealthy
because I did not wish to surrender
my hope of finding trust and the reality of truth
in a culture where nurture and future are at war
with reality and responsibility;
and where the scourge of caste and nostalgia for a glorious,
if not more enlightened, pre-colonial past,
and for a utopia of fundamentalist belief,
cripple the will to modernize and democratize.
The vision of progress and reform is clouded,
subverted by the fear of a loss of power
and a constant source of cheap labor
sustained by pervasive and enduring poverty.
To value equally all peoples
and to give other animals and all living beings
equally fair consideration is the essence of democracy.
But to the commerce and economies of East and West,
whose claim to democracy is hypocrisy at best,
equalitarianism, like egalitarianism, is an abomination.

Perhaps some future child will find a memory,
a story in a coral flake or fallen feather
along the garbage beaches of human history,
or in some ravaged forest hear a lone bird sing,
and ask where has wildness and all beauty gone?
And why? Then find her way.
What of that last human child after the plunder
with nowhere left to hide, or to dream the wild,
to die with a dragonfly at summer's end
and be reborn in a little pond next spring,
sucking the life out of frog-sung, sun-spawned tadpoles
to make rainbows with new wings
shimmering in the dance around her eyes
upon an Earth of sighs and wonder?
Experiencing life in human form
before returning to the source and One in all,
what mark of gratitude
or legacy of the truth I seek to live

might I hope to leave behind?
Have I helped more than I have harmed?
Have I given more than I have taken?
Have I lived more for others than for myself?
Was it all illusion to believe I saw
the sacredness of nature
as the nature of the sacred,
and every creature as a Word of God?
I have been touched by so much
that has moved me from joy to tears,
from the incredulous devotion in a dog's eyes
whom I have healed, to a water buffalo's
soft gaze, and sweet breath, after being rescued
from a death-march to the slaughter house:
From the sight of a captive orphan baby elephant,
her wild mother shot for raiding crops,
dying without love and proper care,
to the shimmering power of a long python
sliding from our arms to jungle freedom.

Between the words, the great silence.
Within the silence, stillness, and motion,
Action, dreaming, repose, and incubation.
By day, I rage against the dying of the Light
and touch the stars at night
in gratitude for having helped another soul
with all I have to offer and to share.
In my repose, I find the words for these elegies
in the rain, songs of whispering leaves and cool frogs,
and in my dreams when the animals speak,
shape-shifting into jungle spirits
like dream tigress' swift attack that I embraced
accepting what is, and what is to be,
and she became a woman entwined
with me in the ecstasy of the living Earth.

Animals are our teachers
when we are open to them;
our guides when we live for them;
our healers when we feel for them;
and our allies when we fight for their rights
because their liberation and ours
are one, as one breath shared.

VIII
Elephants: Broken Spirits, Breaking Hearts

Ganesh's crime was breaking a front tooth
what exquisite precision—in the face
that was inspecting him: The Chief Wildlife Warden's.
This brought shame on his handlers,
and to the elephant camp at Thepakkadu, Nilgiris.
So, he was beaten by twelve men,
for an hour as he screamed, chained by each leg,
to "take out his nuts and bolts,"
they shouted in Tamil,
and they blinded Ganesh in one eye.
After the beating and blinding,
Ganesh was chained and starved for five months.

Later, it was said Ganesh
had poked his eye on a broken branch.
At this same camp, other elephants,
like Subramanian and Vigaia, were beaten
then kept in one place in chains
and starved for many months
for turning on their handlers,
who were often drunk or young and untrained.

Even after being captive for generations,
the elephant has never become domesticated.
At times, they go berserk, attacking keepers,
rampaging through streets and crowds,
or with one swift movement, injure or kill.
Sometimes, they are shot and killed,
but being valuable, most are returned
to a life in chains—that some call a reprieve
after retraining, rehabilitation, and being 'reformed'
continue as circus or temple slaves,
or as beasts of burden, carrying tourists on their backs
and dragging the last trees out of their wild kingdom.
Training methods traditional and new
to break the spirit of the wild
(and you see it gone in elephant eye and aura
—that witnessing I shed tears of fire)
include starvation, confinement in chains and ropes,
electric prods and goads;
the ancient ankus, both spear and tearing hook;

bamboo canes, whips, sticks, clubs, machetes,
and injections of tranquilizers,
under dubious veterinary supervision
at the best of times.

One captured wild elephant,
a 40-year-old Makhna or tuskless bull
whom we named Loki, we witnessed
being beaten with canes by two screaming men
on his terrible leg wounds
for forty-five minutes to make him lie down;
and for how many days later
as we were forbidden to treat him anymore.
The good food that we had given him
was making him too strong,
but he was as gentle as a puppy with us,
and called out to us in greeting
when he heard our jeep.
But he was still too crippled
to ever lie down.
He had been standing in a log crate
unable to walk or easily turn around
for seven months while Deanna's team,
that had been called in to treat his infected wounds,
witnessed and recorded this calculated cruelty
to kill his spirit and make him go down
that had been ordered by the authorities.

Sanctioned by India's most esteemed elephant veterinarian
who felt it was time to break and train him,
Loki was eventually dispirited and enslaved.
His four legs had been cut down
to the tendons, some even severed,
by wires and chains used in his restraint
after chemical, dart-gun capture
and severe goring by five Kumkhis;
trained bull elephants with enormous tusks
used to capture wild elephants
and to subdue 'rogue' elephants in the camp.
These injuries, according to India's top elephant scientist,
"Were post-capture, caused by his struggling."
In other words, all Loki's fault,
and his pus-filled Khumki gore wounds were said
to be from old gunshot wounds.

Three years later, we succeeded in
bringing Loki's story of suffering and abuse
before India's Supreme Court in Delhi.

The saga of this one elephant
will go down in history as the lightning rod
that exposed so much elephant suffering,
vehemently justified by custom and necessity
that was endorsed by some scientists and officials,
who told the press that their veterinarians
had quickly healed the elephant
with a new mixture of barley, honey, and olive oil,
and that Deanna was only making a fuss to raise
a lot of money. Yet for months,
Loki was a mound of pus and spreading infection,
and became a broken, dispirited, permanent cripple
who can never be healed in body, mind, or soul:
A living shadow, but a celebrity at the camp
because his plight became an international concern,
signed on by over thirty members of the US Senate,
and an embarrassment to the Indian government's
spiritual and caring image to the world.

Elephants and other animals, like us, remember,
binding past visions and sensations
to the feelings of their embodied souls.
When we harm their bodies or their spirits,
their souls, scarred forever,
may never fully heal. So, wild elephants
attack, and captive ones go berserk,
or become shadows slowly fading
year after year in chains, if a broken heart
does not kill them sooner.

IX
When All Things Fall Apart, Gather Shadows, Face the Light

Returning to the West after being in the jungle
with the First People of the Third World,
where wild elephants crack and rumble in the bamboo
and panther-spying monkeys scream and chatter close by
as I sleep to the rhythm of Kurumba drums,
later to awaken to the fidelity
of dawn's chorus of uncountable birds
in their daily affirmation and ritual of light,
I feel like a stranger in my own land:
Forever changed, yet having gained
far more than I have lost,
as though coming to my senses;
awakening from a long sleep
induced by a culture and way of life
the rest of the world cannot sustain
if the last of the wild is to remain.
Much that gave me a sense of belonging,
feelings of achievement and purpose
is now lost or transformed
by the unexpected alchemy of passion,
avocation, and longing for the wild.

Yet, I alone cannot save the Nilgiris,
stop the death of nature,
and the holocaust of the animals.
I have borne witness and informed
those who would rather not know
and prefer to work within the status quo
of international conferences, giving money
in the name of human rights, conservation
and animal protection,
to those who, like Nero fiddling while Rome burns,
put radio-collars on wild elephants,
to study why they become crop-raiders,
are awarded international prizes for conservation,
being given more money to do more of the same
but they fear to confront the politics of
tribal, tiger, and elephant extinction;
and those who raise vast sums 'exposing' animal cruelty,
then do nothing more than seek legislative
and regulatory reforms of practices causing animal suffering,

that conscience and common sense
would seek instead to outlaw, East and West, forever.

Those who so profit from the plight of exploited animals,
wild and tame, and of tribal peoples,
are anathema to the ethics of compassion
and reverence for the life they purport to protect.
I have been told by many, young and old,
that humanity can never change
and be humane, because cruelty and indifference
are part of human nature, inborn
like the killing instinct of lion and wolf.
"Look at human history," they say,
"What's the point in bashing your head
against a wall; fighting for justice and reform,
people will never change."

But if it is mere selfishness and ignorance
that make us inhumane, cruel, and indifferent,
then surely, we can learn that altruism
is the most enlightened form of selfishness,
and pure selfishness is simple ignorance.
So informed, we can then choose obedience
to the Golden Rule, and flourish beside lion and wolf,
or suffer the karma of arrested evolution,
and the eternal round of suffering and despair
from age to age that we deserve.

Lack of reason, empathy, and conscience
can be no excuse, nor hatred, rage, or fear.
What, if from age to age
we see so little progress, hope,
as human numbers multiply
and the Golden Rule means simply
those who have the gold shall rule,
and those without shall slowly perish?
What, if from age to age
there is no real change and we remain
forever a chimeric form,
half angelic, half demonic
in the limbo of a heavenly hell?

Does that preclude compassion in action,
simple deeds of loving kindness
to those in greater need than we?
No one alone can change the world,
but we each alone can help and care,
for we are free to choose

and dare to look the beggar in the eye,
and share our bread with dog and God.

Beyond despair, we have our love
for all, and sufferings to share,
becoming strong in knowing
we are not alone.

X
The Outsiders from Nemesis to Apotheosis

Blind to the spirit in the flesh,
in the leaf, in the stone,
the psychosis of chauvinism
means no Thing has inherent worth
and is empty of spirit.
Being blind to this and that
where there is no outside
(for all Things are within),
the Outsider can never
be inside another, like lovers
in feeling with each other,
but instead condemned to exile
forever on the outside
from one life to the next.

When Outsiders speak to me,
their words make no pictures
and I feel and see nothing.
My mind begins to spin
in the vacuum of nothingness;
reaches for the clarity of Earth-speak
in the syllables of rustling leaves
and forest voices from the cathedral stillness
of ancient trees and high peaks.
Making no pictures for lack of vision
or is their vision so alien,
from some other dimension
of heartless separation?
the Outsiders become indistinguishable
from the living dead,
deaf to the language

of the trees they cut and truck away,
and the silence that remains
wherever they have been.

The Outsiders cannot see nature's
often terrifying beauty transfigured
in the reflection of the infinite;
the divine presence of the Absolute,
the *mysterium tremendum*.
Not seeing life as miraculous
how can they ever revere
the sanctity of every life
and all that sustains and renews?

How can they be moved by the sacred
to respect the holiness of being,
until all the suffering they cause
and fear and fail to feel, eventually
wears them down, and they are drawn
by gentle wings and forgiving hands
toward the heart and truth and home of all
where there is harmony, a kind of peace,
and wholeness, with no Outsiders.

Without wilderness, the life of the mind
is impoverished, unrefined, defined
by monoculture; human-centered.
How then can we atone for being human?
How else except through the heart of all:
In wildness is the recovery of humanity.
Then we may see the consequences
and connections of global warming,
war, disease, poverty
and the silence of the frogs;
and find the cure for cancer
in our communion and healing of the Earth:
And appreciate the prophecy
that the sky will fall when the trees are gone.
We all could come together so easily
with clarity of mind and purity of heart
under the banner of mutual aid
where there are no Outsiders to the sacred whole.

What god-man sat beneath a tree
and said, "This is it!" as he became
a child of feeling, one with all,
womb within womb, being within being,
on a beaming smile of light?

The same who said,
"When you put the outside on the inside,
and the inside on the outside,
than you will enter the Kingdom of Heaven."

The Outsiders are the living dead,
who only exist inside themselves,
just for themselves, forever strangers
to wonder, mystery, and impartial love.
There are no Outsiders when our lips are dust
and the flight of albatross and Arctic tern
follow the contours of our hearts
in the deep interior of Angels' dreams.

You will know when you have crossed over,
forever changed by the stain of evil,
with that thousand-yard stare
from the heartbreak of perpetual war.
Part of you remains on a distant shore
so all the norms and satisfactions of returning home
and the familiar enjoyments and cherishing
become surreal; you feel alone, broken,
and hollow as an eagle bone.
The nice and the good and the comfortable
whose shadows bear no stain,
stay clean, as uninvolved as floating leaves,
never having crossed into the realm
of pure evil, and the endless war.
To fight or die; to kill or be killed
the choices of the wild,
nature's amoral quantum field.
We can fight for the freedom
to live and let live,
and not to have to kill
or cause so much suffering,
when we acknowledge evil's presence,
and would rather die than kill,
for all that we believe and hold so dear.

Jungle morning comes like a soft fawn
moving silently out of the night
on silver hooves of dew into the sun
that turns twilight crimson, violet and gold.
As the dawn sky rises and opens
the trees begin to shimmer, their silhouettes
condensing out of the velvet dark
beneath the morning star, slowly fading into blue.
In every jungle morning walking meditation

or standing contemplation, I found
inspiration and affirmation in nature's presence
that drew my spirit out and gave it wings.

But my soul burned with bitter tears
for her vulnerability and relentless pillage
by those I would face by end of day:
Those who spread lies, disinformation,
slander and xenophobia,
because our work to help the poor,
their animals, and to support conservation
and rule of law, threatened vested interests
and the status quo of a nexus of power,
corruption and abuse of office.

The backlash from quarters threatened and shamed,
was calculated to harm our reputation and integrity.
Being cumulative, it became dispiriting
until we saw we were at war; good against evil,
compassion against cruelty; rule of law
against injustice and abuse of power.
One false rumor was that I was getting rich
testing experimental drugs on village dogs.

Another, widely spread by a government minister,
was that we were profiting royally
"On the backs of India's suffering animals,"
through fund-raising appeals,
and that our animal refuge was in reality
our private country retreat,
with a few animals kept just for show.
Perhaps the day would bring another death threat,
police harassment, official investigation,
or more rumors of pending arrest,
visa revocation and deportation
to silence us in the endless war
against corruption, cruelty, and greed.

But Deanna endured to save the life and beauty
of this sacred place where still
the dream of the Earth is evident
In the pulse of insects in the night,
rumbling elephants, tigers' huffs, and chuffs,
and morning bird song that fills our hearts.

The 'Empathosphere' and Compassion's Light

Without empathy, there can be no coherent ethical basis for society, and no moral consistency in our lives and in our relationships within the broader life community of the planetary ecosystem. In many ways, non-human animals are more empathically connected and aware than humans.

They are more attuned to each other and to their immediate environment, a vital survival strategy being less self-preoccupied and lost in thought than we, which could have fatal consequences in the wild. As we become ever more deeply connected through empathic knowledge and associated feeling, we enter the empathosphere, or realm of fellow-feeling and understanding.

In this realm, our consciousness becomes reflexive, conscience and consciousness are born and we become a more caring, whole, and healthy species, culture, community, family and person.

In my book, *The Boundless Circle,* where I first outlined my initial understanding of the empathosphere, I linked it with the boundless ethic of compassion. This boundlessness is evident in the invisible ripple-effect of good works or some new idea spreading from community to community.

Two animals demonstrated the boundless nature of the empathosphere at the animal refuge in the Nilgiris, South India established by my wife, Deanna Krantz. Somehow, they knew that the refuge was a place of security and relief from suffering.

How else to explain these two animals coming several miles to where they had never been before? One was a dog whom we called Whitey, who dragged himself after being hit by a vehicle for over a mile to the refuge with a broken back and with his testicles hanging out.

Another was a water buffalo whom staff found one morning waiting at the refuge gate. Her condition was quickly recognized and treated, which was an infected vagina seething with flesh-eating maggots.

One dog at Deanna's refuge, Bruno, would insist on observing every surgery being performed on an animal and would lie attentively beside them during their recovery. Mania, an adult Bonnet macaque monkey, gently held an infant monkey while being treated for burns after swinging on electrified wires.

Mania the 'monkey nurse', dog Bruno caring for just-spayed Vigia. Monkeys playing with Whitey.

The mourning of elephants over the remains of their herd-mates has been well documented, and many witnessed the most recent account of African elephants paying tribute to conservationist, Lawrence Anthony. According to *The Ark, Journal of Catholic Concern for Animals*, (No.222, Autumn/Winter 2012):

"Two days after he died in March 2012, a herd of wild elephants, led by two matriarchs, arrived at his home, followed by separate wild herds-a total of 20 elephants in all, walking over 12 miles to get to his home. Lawrence's widow, Francoise, was especially touched, knowing that the elephants had not been to his house prior to that day for well over a year. Yet, they knew where they were going. They stayed there for two days and two nights."

Deanna with rescued mule from the war in Kashmir (left); (right) the author returns after leave of absence to the refuge, and is greeted by the dogs with Dean, pack leader in his arms.

One of the most celebrated and phenomenal feats of empathic 'sixth-sense' finding of a loved one occurred during World War I. It involved an Irish terrier named Prince journeying from England in late September after his master had been sent with his battalion across the sea to Europe that August.

Several weeks later, Prince found his master in the trenches in Flanders, France. (For details, see Neil R. Storey, *Animals in the First World War*, Shire Publications UK, 20014).

In the US, the story of seven-year-old Samoyed-husky mix dog named Zander hit the news media in early October 2012. Somehow, she was able to find her beloved master, John Dolan, suffering in the Good Samaritan Hospital in Islip, NY, a difficult two miles from her home that included crossing a stream, a highway and tricky navigation through neighborhood streets where she had never been before.

Good Morning America reporter, Avianne Tan, posted the account on 13 February 2015 of Sissy, an 11-year-old miniature Schnauzer in Cedar Rapids, Iowa, who ended up at Mercy Medical Center 20 blocks from her home where her co-owner, Nancy Frank, was recovering from cancer surgery.

A surveillance camera in the hospital lobby caught the dog entering through the automatic doors and wandering around. Husband Dale Franck finally got a call at 5:30 am from a security officer who found his phone number and house address from the dog's collar tag.

Dale Franck's daughter got permission to take Sissy up to Nancy Franck for a few minutes, he said. His theory about how Sissy might have gotten 20 blocks to his wife was that Sissy used to ride with him to pick up his wife from work next door to the hospital, but they had never walked that route before.

These and other remarkable instances of animal empathy and understanding have confirmed for me the reality, complexity and beauty of the empathosphere. Scientist Rupert Sheldrake has empirical evidence of the existence of the empathosphere, which he calls a morphic field.

Animals' resonance with this field enables them, for example, to know when their owners are coming home. Within this realm of being and feeling is awareness that all things are connected. This means that when we, humans, harm another sentient being, the harm may not be limited to that one being.

There is a ripple-effect and others feel and know, just like the ripple-effect of loving concern and compassion in action at the refuge that injured and sick animals, through remote or distance-sensing, could feel and so find their way to the refuge for treatment.

The ripple effects following the harpooning of whales, and the incarceration and suffering of animals in factory farms and research laboratories, may be far more pervasive and no less real than the anguish caring people feel for all creatures who are treated inhumanely and unjustly by those who are disconnected in heart and mind from others' suffering and joy, and from the sanctity of being.

I feel blessed indeed by the opportunity to be able to help other animals in need. Seeing the look of terror and despair in a dog's eyes melt into trust and gratitude after days of treatment by our devoted staff at Deanna's Animal Refuge was one of the greatest rewards.

Seeing our resident animals interacting with others in recovery and showing care and concern, gentleness and understanding, provides me with a deeper appreciation of animal awareness and sensitivity. Then to see them play, some for the first time—for the first time not starving, or in pain, or afraid and thus being free to express and experience the joy of being.

To see their spirits gain free expression and their personalities blossom in the safe and loving environment of the refuge borders on the miraculous. As we become more mindful of the consequences of how we regard and treat other animals, the power of loving concern through compassionate action will be the catalyst for our evolution and transformation into a truly humane species, for the good of all.

Empathy brings the light of human compassion into the world that is part of that ineffable light that is transfiguring, transforming, and transcending. As the Buddha advised, the only true religion is *maitri* (loving kindness or benevolence) toward all creatures. He also taught that the end of suffering is in suffering itself—through empathy.

There is a wonderful story of a Buddhist monk who did not become enlightened until he put compassion into action. Geshe Kelsang Gyatso writes:

> Asanga, a Great Buddhist Master who lived in India in the fifth century AD, meditated in an isolated mountain cave to gain a vision of Buddha Maitreya. After twelve years, he still had not succeeded and, feeling discouraged, abandoned his retreat.
> On his way down the mountain, he came across an old dog lying in the middle of the path. Its body was covered in maggot-infested sores, and it seemed close to death. This sight induced within Asanga an overwhelming feeling of compassion for all living beings trapped within samsara.
> As he was painstakingly removing the maggots from the dying dog, it suddenly transformed into Buddha Maitreya himself. Maitreya explained that he had been with Asanga since the beginning of his retreat, but due to the impurities in Asanga's mind, Asanga had not been able to see him.
> It was Asanga's extraordinary compassion that had finally purified the karmic obstructions preventing him from seeing Maitreya.

Light, enlightenment, wisdom and compassion are interwoven phenomena and concepts evident in the world's major religions that are linked with divine revelation and presence. In the *Taittiriya Upanishad,* for example, it is written: "May the light of sacred knowledge illumine us, and may we attain the glory of wisdom." (1.3)

But there is also the light of love and compassion, as implied in the *Chandogya Upanishad:* "There is a Light that shines beyond all things on earth, beyond us all, beyond the heavens, beyond the highest, the very highest heavens. This is the Light that shines in our hearts." (3:13.7)

The three central themes of the *Bhagavad Gita* are *jnana, bhakti* and *karma* (light, love and life). In Buddhism, we also find reference to the Light as a reflection of Buddha-nature, and in Christianity, the halos of saints represent the radiance of divine nature.

The 13th-century Sufi poet, Jalalu'l Din Rumi, advised, "If you keep your gaze fixed upon the Light, you will be delivered from dualism and the plurality of the finite body."

In more recent times, Martin Luther King wrote, "Every man must decide whether he will walk in the light of creative altruism or the darkness of destructive selfishness."

Light, enlightenment, wisdom and compassion are interwoven phenomena and concepts evident in the world's major religions that are linked with as a scientist, I have always had a healthy skepticism and curiosity about the phenomenology of 'The Light'. Reported studies of auras, Kirlian photography, and other approaches taken by the material sciences to quantify what others believe to be non-material, spiritual or purely subjective, do little to prove, disprove or enhance our understanding of the Light.

A few years before, I was witness to the Light in India in association with animals, I was sent a photograph of a Tibetan Buddhist monk blessing the animals. Along with this photograph came the following explanation:

> *In July 1985, the first Phowa course by the Ven. K. C. Ayang Rinpoche was held in Tokyo, Japan. After the course, Rinpoche made a short visit to holy places in Kyoto and Nara, the ancient capitals of Japan. On the 26th July, a photo was taken of Rinpoche with some deer in Nara Park. When the photo was developed, a clear rainbow appeared on the print. Many people have asked about the photo and this is the background to it. On that day, many photos were taken in the park but I clearly remember taking this one as Rinpoche went and sat with the deer and said, "Take a photo now." This was the only time that he had asked for a photo to be taken.*
>
> *After the photo was developed, I asked Rinpoche why he thought the rainbow had appeared and what it could mean. He told me that while he was sitting with the deer, he had been strongly wishing that they could all go directly to the Buddha Amitabha Pure Land after this life and that the Buddha Amitabha would make contact with them from that moment.*
>
> *It is his belief that the Buddha Amitabha made contact with the deer at the time the picture was taken and that the power of His blessing appeared in rainbow form (see photo below).*
>
> *At the time the photo was taken, no rainbow was visible and there was no rain. It was a clear, sunny afternoon and none of the other photos had any rainbows or light effects although all were taken under the same light conditions within a short space of time.*
>
> *It is also interesting that the place where the photo was taken, Nara Park, is considered to be sacred ground and the meeting point of several 'ley lines' (lines of energy in the earth that seem to be linked with the location of major holy sites and buildings).*
>
> *This park contains three of Japan's most revered shrines and temples, including Todaiji, an important Buddhist temple famous for its huge statue of the Buddha Vairocana.*
>
> *Rinpoche believes the real presence of the Buddha Amitabha is with this photo and has said, "I am praying that whoever keeps this photo with strong confidence and devotion will become inseparable with the Buddha Amitabha's mercy and compassion." (Jackie Young, The Rainbow Photograph of the Ven. K.C. Ayang Rinpoche)*

Ven. K.C. Ayang Rinpoche blessing the deer at Nara Park, 26 July 1985

With no intent to emulate, though I was deeply moved by the vision of the rainbow that is the spectral vision of the Buddha-light of divine presence, I was no less touched by some of the photographs of my humble self, enjoying the blessings of communion with a water buffalo, the emissaries from a herd of donkeys, and a billy-goat.

These, and a total of some 200 animal souls, enjoyed the security and freedom from fear and hunger in Deanna's animal refuge. This peaceable kingdom was a creation of loving compassion and years of dedicated hard work under inconceivably difficult circumstances.

The light of India does not shine very bright for most animals. In these photographs, I saw what I felt at the time; a golden light, sometimes with a whitish haze, almost dazzling, yet tender, around the animals. I recalled seeing at times the entire animal refuge and staff suffused in this light that was omnipresent and intensified just before dusk, when alpha dog Dean would have me meditate.

I knew the light I was witnessing was for real. I had seen it go out after Deanna and some ninety animals were forced out from a defunct animal shelter that she had been invited to restore—but the community did not expect her to confront the endemic animal suffering, cruelty, corruption, and wildlife decimation in the surrounding jungle.

Of course, she did confront all these issues, along with the Jains who were using the animal shelter to house spent cows to slowly starve to death because euthanasia was a violation of the principle of ahimsa, (non-harming), and compassionate killing would make the perpetrators 'spiritually impure' and got into much trouble for her good labors.

I realized that the Light had gone when I went back to the defunct sanctuary to pick up a few remaining items after Deanna and most of the animals had been forced out. I was so surprised that I got out of the jeep to look. The sky was clear and sunny, but all the vegetation, the earth, and the buildings had turned almost gray; everything seemed flat, tired, lacking in radiance and vitality.

Most of the birds had already left to relocate to her new refuge just across the little river no more than 300 yards away, where there was food, water and sanctuary for all. I remembered, as I stood there in disbelief in this dispirited place, that I had seen the same loss of light in the captive elephants in American zoos and circuses, and at a nearby elephant camp.

Compared to those in the wild who roamed nearby, it was quite apparent that these poor elephants had lost their radiance and vitality. Clearly, my senses had revealed to me a phenomenon about which I had had no prior intimation as either part of my education or culture.

The consequences of compassionate care are indeed profound, teaching me another way of seeing, if not another dimension of life. I will be forever grateful for the happy and secure creatures at Deanna's refuge who embraced me in the Light, and of course, to Deanna.

Sometimes, a camera will catch the images which our rational minds of such experiences would deny, like the rainbow that appeared when a Tibetan monk was blessing some deer in a park in Japan.

My rendition of a vision that I experienced in the ancient St. Oran's Chapel near the abbey on the Isle of Iona on the west coast of Scotland invokes a sense of the numinous for some, an affirmation that this world is but one reality of which there are many dimensions, including the manifestations of our loved ones—human and non-human—after their mortal existence has come to its end. So soon will ours.

Vision on the Isle of Iona in St. Oran's Chapel, July 1958

Collected Poems 1975–2024

I
If Fish Could Scream

I had a dream
That fish could scream.
So there were no fishermen
For none could bear to hear
The screams of netted fish
Or tolerate the painful cries
Of those impaled on spear and hook.
Did God give silence to the fish
That we might never hear nor feel
Their fear and pain,
Just so we can eat them
With no twinge of shame
Or fellow-feeling?
We might ask what kind
Of God makes all fish mute
Who in their silence,
Suffer suffocation in our trawler nets,
Pain and terror on our hooks?
Perhaps that we might learn
To feel through silence
For the mute, the weak, the dumb,
Of our kind and fish kind
And all kind great and small.

August 1985
Published in *Between the Species* magazine.

II
The Panther

Just before my thirteenth birthday
I joined the spirit of a captive panther
As she paced and rubbed herself red raw
Against a polished tree stump with every turn
Making tracks and patinas of blood
Around her iron and concrete universe.
As I stood beside a potted palm
In the glass domed conservatory
At the Paris zoo, Le Jardin des Plantes,
I saw the bars through her eyes
Spinning to the cadence of her measured minuet
As she slowly ground herself into the final freedom
Of death and liberation with graceful deliberation.
Perhaps the spinning took away her pain.
Through her mesmerized, hypnotic gaze
I saw through the haze of my tears
Gray shadow people passing oblivious,
While she writhed like a black serpent
In the slow suicide of her repetitive motion
Under the compulsion of wildness for freedom
To end all of her spirit's longing and soul's desire.
Then I saw the bars were also around the people
Who never stopped to look and see and care.
I felt closer to my panther and her pain and fate
Than to my own kind so blind to her tragic plight.
When I left the panther to her chosen end,
In broken French, I asked a keeper to take me
To the director of the zoo menagerie
In the urban heart of gay Paris in 1950.
The keeper led me to the official's office
Through a maze of glass cases
Filled with stuffed and pickled creatures
From every continent and sea.
Up several flights of marble stairs
I met the man in charge
Who waved his hands and said,
"What can we do? That is how she is."

Half a century later, I read Rilke's poem
About a panther in the same plight and place.
I wonder how many lived and died that way
In the century between our visits

And for why. Was it ten, twenty or more
Who were tortured in that corner cage?

Suffering the severance of living souls
From all wildness, being, purpose,
I find such zoos, like the animal circus
Make me alien to my species, and ashamed.

August 2004

III
Bovine Ruminations

I remember that sweet vision
Of cows quietly grazing
When I was deep thinking
In the time of my youth
Of what I should do with my life.
When the cows began glowing
In my searching mind's eye
As the bus sped me by,
I knew what to do; what I'm doing
Right now to recall
The cows in the meadow and the god in all.

Sad the trusting cow
Torn of her calf
And calling all the night.
Let us pray.

Lost the innocent calf
In his narrow crate
And fattening for the plate.
Let us pray.

Goaded the weary ox
Bearing our loads
And ploughing all the day.
Let us pray.

Bloody the noble bull
Dying in the ring
And bellowing heaven's rage.
Let us pray.

February 1987.
First published in *In Newer Veins: An Anthology of Poetry Written by Veterinary Surgeons.* A. R. Mitchell & E. Boden, (eds.) 1998.

IV
They Came Down from the Trees

Complete in themselves,
Safe and secure, the monkeys
Kept to the trees, wanting no more.
Their needy cousins came down
Learned to make fire,
Turned stones into iron
For ploughs and for war.
So different they were
From those in the trees,
Calling themselves human,
Self-anointing above all else,
Homo sapiens, man the wise.

So clever indeed,
Playing god with atoms and genes
Laying waste to the old world
To make way for the new.

September 2008

V
I Knew a Child

I knew a child who looked
Into the eyes of animals,
And saw the self in others:

A child who learned the language
Of the trees and spoke to rocks;
Could fly on clouds and dream.

Born to know through feeling,
Children flourish or perish:
So too the animals.

What world we make for ours
And theirs, can blind in pain
Or bind in light to love.
I knew a child who saw the light
And felt all pain but shone
With joy in love for all.
Uncorrupted like eternal spring
The child within moves on,
Secure in a universe embraced.

In grace and wonder,
Innocent and selflessness,
This child is parent to us all.

February 2007

VI
God Right, God Wrong

Have you found the God of little things?
Felt divinity around, within
The awe inspiring miracle of life
In the dream that is dreaming us?
Have you the right god, and I the wrong?
Better, then, for all to have none.
In what god's name have many killed,
Been killed, tortured and oppressed;
Converted and perverted?
In what God's name have many loved,
Been healed, made whole;
Redeemed and reconciled?
Some say the way to God
Is the way of peace and renunciation.
Renounce all gods of our own making,
Created in our own vain image,
Along with hatred, greed and fear
But not the God of little things.
Separated from belief and disbelief
We discover divinity within each other.
The truth that sets us free to serve.
To heal and to make whole
Through our sense of the sacred,
In the sanctity of silent oaks
And standing stones.

September 2008

VII
New Year Reflections

When love, suffering, service
Are one, there is grace within;
Arrogance and fear are gone.

When fear and hatred are one
With arrogance and power,
There is peace and joy for none.

Human spirit, Earth are one.
The worlds we make
Reflect and shape the soul.

Unspoken dread, living
With the dead forgotten,
Blinds us to the sacred deep

Where soul-mates meet
In sanctuary to sanctify
Life and death in trust and love.

Compassionate service is all
Amidst inhuman-kind's demise
And the great awakening to care.

In a world of suffering
What pleasure can there be
Except to serve, help heal?
No time to wonder if you are loved
Or are unlovable, or if your wants
Are childhood longings unfulfilled.
A broken heart, a broken world,
Call for every able soul
To see and feel and know
The end of suffering from ignorance,
Arrogance, hatred, fear,
Is in simple acts of loving kindness
To all beings great and small
Whom we embrace in reverence
And suffer all to come to us.

January 2008

VIII
Coming to Sioux Falls, S. Dakota

Prairie, plains, all torn;
The blight of cattle, corn.
Poisoned streams.
Suicidal dreams.
Dead bitch in ditch,
Car-flat possums, 'coons
Cardboard cat cut-outs
Pave my highway.
Soft feet of Sioux,
Buffalo ghosts echo silence.
All the taker's money gained
Will never be sustained.
Not worth a tinker's cuss.
Renunciation a distant call
To hallow all,
So glad coyotes sing.

September 2007

IX
August Evening

Reaching out now, this soft summer eve,
as tree frogs and crickets symphonize
to call up storms, or peace, in the voice
of many in the heart of One,
I find the root connections of my being.
I become their tree; their song and night,
and they, my doorway, senses,
guides to show us all the way:
The way of seers and prophets,
Shamans' journeys into ancestral realms
primordial, protean thoughts,
as well the boundless source of all wisdom
that inspires our art, informs our science:
And illumes all life.

August 2006

X
Flying Not Away

Oozing out into unintelligible realms
where the mind is jangled into mush,
the wandering soul is set adrift,
severed from all broken hearts.
The endless journey starts
when there is no home, no returning.
Only the outward flow, an expanding universe,
gathering its past, all riches,
cherished memories and pain.
All remorse and regret remain
forever buried under glaciers of time.
With no hope, there is no future:
Only an eternity of heaven in hell.

Flying not away, but toward
the destination of an open heart,
following the song lines
of air churned wings
and more ancient souls
into tomorrow, another season,
to find the place of all abiding
grace and peace: A consummation
devoutly wished, ordained
by wild spirits, Earth bound, yet free.
Free to serve without servitude,
the snow geese sing antiphonal anthems
as they pass above me in this vibrant night
into some new day where I am waiting
beyond the curve of light
to welcome them in silent gratitude.

December 2005

XI
Healing the Rain

Everywhere the rain burns into soft skins
and tender leaves and wings, poisoning all
once nurtured and sustained. Nothing is immune,
or can be cleansed and healed by waters once so pure,
without the tears of angels and wisdom's loving care.

Who in human or other mortal form suffers for the rain,
must bear the pain of all. All suffering is one.
All beings strive and rise toward the Light
they cherish, nurture and sustain.
Each becomes, as grass or elephant, tree or man,
the mother, midwife, giver to a living Earth.

Through them the All is manifest:
Immanent and omnipresent,
until blind hearts evolve to poison the rain,
not feeling the good in all and all in good;
not treating water as their mother, sister
lover, brother—the Sacred Other in the rain.
Only what they see is real; feelings are unreal.
The rains will continue to anoint us with our sins
until we wash away the veil of separation.
For are we not all water beings?
When we harm the skies, we harm ourselves.
Our finer feelings, like the wind, we must trust
to inform and guide our own emergence
into the Light of wisdom, beauty and gratitude.
April, 2005

XII
The Beast Within

Thinly veiled as civilized
The beast within remains contained.
Outsiders think it tame.

Well-trained, the child becomes the man,
Respected citizen, father of two:
Two more beasts to be contained.

Well-trained for circus life,
They act upon command
Or crack their whips and smiles.

Knowing not what freedom is,
The beast is tamed, and life goes on.
Some break out; such calamity.

From one insanity into another
More primal, urgent, cruel,
For the beast within was never held
Nor loved. So it grew, deformed,
Contained within, beneath the carapace
Of saving face and civic pride.

No place to hide from naked truth
The beast within consumes itself
And men are broken, empty shells.

July 2007

XIII
In Wildness

In wildness, we find the sum of all our fears and longing
Where feral hearts beat Earth drums into ecstatic revelation
Through dance and song, and trance of insight
On shimmering leaves, rippling streams, eyes of wolves
And our shadow-souls, vibrant, trembling at the openings
Of cave and consciousness. Some scream, rant and rave,
So intense the power of truth, dismembering lies;
Then retreat into the security of the known.

In wildness is all we fear, revere and sanctify.
Dream-makers and earth-breakers make war
Because they share no feeling, vision, understanding.
One destroys while the other nurtures and sustains.
One species of two minds cuts a whole world in two.

Now, wildness is defiled, domesticated, civilized, commercialized
By mammonists deluded by self-righteousness and entitlement.
But with the authority of empathic wisdom we could make
A world where beauty and justice are incorruptible twins,
For the plight and suffering of one is felt and shared by all.
The wordless wild speaks to us in many tongues.
When we learn the language of the trees
And all creatures great and small,
We will make right our many wrongs.

October 2005

XIII Becoming

An eagle's first flight is into freedom from fear
Where resistance and supplication resonate
Like lovers elemental, ancient and wise
In the sacred union of wings and air.
As her feathers sing she soars and cries,
Circling the mountain's echoes of affirmation
Of the miracle and ecstasy of being.
Who would tear the eagle from the sky
With gun and arrow or poisoned bait?
No one can possess such beauty
Or annihilate such power
To rob the Earth
Of yet another child
And impoverish our souls and world.
The eagles of the skies teach us
How to take the leap and fly
Empowered by the love of life
Beyond blind trust, hope and faith,
Not pinioned by fear and self-doubt,
To become the wind, the rain, a tree, a wolf.
In the sanctity, all these beings of our becoming
We can reclaim our humanity and sanity.

May 2014

XIV
A Prayer for My Species

Where there is discord, let there be concord.
Where there is chaos and insanity, let there be equanimity.
Where there is hatred and rage, let there be reason.
Where there is betrayal, let there be restitution.
Where there is nothing to live for, let there be something to die for.
Where there is passion, let there be self-restraint.
Where there is love, let there be selflessness.
Where there is power, let there be service for the greater good.
Where there is wealth, let there be generosity.
Where there is harm, let there be repentance.
Where there is lying, let there be the courage of confession.
Where there is deception, let there be worthy intention.
Where there is justice, let there be impartiality.
Where there is law, let there be equal justice.
Where there is morality, let there be ethical sensibility.
Where there is wrath, let there be lawful constraint.
Where there is war, let there be the constraint of sanity.
Where there is victory, let there be mercy.
Where there is ignorance, let there be empathic instruction.
Where there is procreation, let there be moderation.
Where there is death and decay, let there be life renewed.
Where there is suffering, let there be sympathy and relief.
Where there is sickness let there be understanding.
Where there is disease, let there be prevention.
Where there is greed, let there be philanthropy and security.
Where there is lust, let there be tender restraint and release.
Where there is gluttony, let there be consuming acts of loving service.
Where there is slothfulness, let there be passion for life and living.
Where there is depravity, let there be the gravity of good conscience.
Where there is despair, let there be the light of hope.
Where there is sorrow, let there be the light of love.
Where there is fear, let there be courage.
Where there is certainty, let there be caution.
Where there is urgency, let there be foresight.
Where there is ambition, let there be right heart and right mind.
Where there is autonomy, let there be responsibility.
Where there is duty to serve, let there be self-discipline and dignity.
Where there is arrogance, let there be humility and mutual respect.
Where there is prejudice, let there be tolerance and trust.
Where there is vanity, let there be modesty and self-effacement.
Where there is selfishness, let there be feeling for others.
Where there is intolerance, let there be patience and forbearance.

Where there is trust, let there be wide-eyed caution.
Where there is corruption, let there be accountability.
Where there is injustice, let there be full recompense.
Where there is faith, let there be reason and truth.
Where there is religion, let there be tolerance and harmlessness.
Where there is obedience, let there be honor and trust.
Where there is cruelty, let there be compassionate intervention.
Where there is neglect, let there be admonishment and instruction.
Where there is non-human life, let there be reverential respect.
Where there is beauty, let there be contemplation and celebration.
Where there is sentience, let there be communion.

March 2015

XV
An Ode to Christmas Trees

Who mourns with me the little evergreens
By the millions severed
From their roots, so soon to die?
This sacrificial massacre
Of mindless Christmas commerce
Dispirited, dismembering:
Few remembering pagan times
Of solstice celebration, ritual hallowing
The Tree of Life left whole,
Holy and enduring age to age.

"When the trees are gone, the sky will fall,"
is a native American Indian prophesy.
Make Christmas X-mas for these trees
With rituals to restore an ever-greener world.

To save or plant one little tree
Is a better ritual for an enlightened age
Revering all that lives on Earth.

January 2012

XVI
Going Fishing

Before you go fishing or eat a fish,
Take a swim in their schools and shoals.
As their shimmering sides and colors
Suffuse your being you may find
The one mind in many and in the many
Become one. Then go deeper
To join the more solitary ones
Where the pressing silence
Births past and future, ancient forms
You recognize in dreams and in your bones.
If you retain these memories
Returning to your terrestrial domain
You may refrain from eating your relations
From the deep and weep for them,
Then celebrate your contribution
To securing their abiding presence.
Beneath the surfaces of water, earth,
Skin, scale, shell, feather and fur
The power of the world dwells and spells
The words and beauty of Earth's creation.
In the beginning was The Word.
Only we can either mute the world
Or let every sentient being sing.

May 2014

XVII
The Green People

Our blood from Earth's iron heart
Is red with the air we share
Thanks to all things green
The grasses, trees, and those unseen,
In a world where stones become our bones
And the rains all life sustains
Come coursing through our veins.
But blood we spill and few dare care.
Green people and their wolves may soon be gone.
Who will then remember all were one?

September 2013

XVIII
For the Love of Wolves

For some, the wolf is brother,
Sacred other, she-wolf dear,
Perfect mother, wolf song
Kindling the wild in human hearts.
Teacher, totem, kindred spirit
To the First People, a mirror clear
Reflecting self-in-other
From another nation
In life's circle shared by all.

For others more removed,
Word and song of wolf bring fear.
The big bad wolf is near!
Childhood's innocence, empathy,
Openness of heart and mind
To wildness, mystery,
Are disturbed, confused
By nursery rhymes, folklore, fable—
The big bad wolf is here!
Child souls severed from the whole
Where all held sacred is secure,
Grow willing to conform,
To not believe the heart,
Trust the wisdom of the wild,
Respect and honor the sanctity
Of wolves and other nations.
Adulthood comes into the broken circle
With no rites of passage, initiation,
Except to dominate, persecute and kill.
Wolves mourn when pack mates die,
Sisters, brothers, mothers, fathers,
In the pleasure-quest of trophy hunters,
Trappers seeking the perfect pelt to sell
Imbued with suffering no wearer felt.
In such wanton slaughter of the wolf,
We sacrifice compassion, dignity, humility,
In ignorance of how the love
Of wolves once made us human.

Language is perception, revealing
Whatever truths we live by.
Seeing the wolf in splintered ways

The Second People with no unified sensibility
Call the wolf a savage beast, livestock killer,
Carnivorous predator, biological specimen,
Renewable resource, harvested furbearer,
Hunter's trophy, trapper's challenge,
Icon of wilderness, endangered species.
But for the First People, the Anishinaabe,
Ma'iingan, the wolf is of the heart
And spirit shared before all words,
One Soul, one Earth, one Truth revered.

October 2012

XIX
Advice to Brother Wolf

In fear and frenzy,
You try to bite the stars;
My brother, bite away
Your toes instead,
And leave no more than claws
For trapper's jaws.
You hunger, brother
And the bait seems sweet.
Look close and see coyote
Bloated in the bushes,
And smell the fear
That dying bobcat left.
It was for you, my brother.
Go away from here
And in your dreams, eat out
The sadness in my heart.

March 1974

XX
Thee Kill

Soft gray wolf dawn
Glides over the hill,
In silence spills
Into the glade
And tenses;
A warm, dappled shadow
Never senses
The stalking form
Quiet as morning coming
That hides and shifts
From bush to bush:
The sudden rush
Like daybreak is not felt
As the fawn falls softly
Into sunlight
Where wolf eats and rests.

April 1975

XXI
Hunters of the North

We are always on the move
Loping easily
From space to space
Across a timeless snowfield.
We are the shadow hunters
Of the Arctic night
Who sleep in drifting snow
And dance upon the ice.
We are the voice of summer
That lasts no longer
Than the melting of our echoes
In the soft green flush of tundra life.
This is the time when hunters rest,
When cubs are born and fawns
Of deer, and moose and caribou
Thrive on sun-spawned greenery.
Soon, they will be digging in the snow
And ranging out for miles
For what now lies
Rich and lush around them.
They eat for us.
If only all of us could rest together
Feast on sunlight,
There would be no need to kill,
To always be moving into winter.

March 1975

XXII
For Ma'iingan (Ojibwe): Brother Wolf

Once we knew the God of wolves.
Now, dogs worship those
Unworthy, killing wolves.
Wolves with no fear of me
Sang when I blew my flute
Showing me their God
I now worship in my dog.

Michael W. Fox
September 2024

XXIII
Lamentation of the Larks

Where have all the meadow larks gone?
They filled my childhood's soul
When they spiraled and trilled above me
In the rapture of a living world
As I lay concealed in dancing grass.

Gone too the swifts, swallows, moonbeam bats
Some insects flourish, immune to pesticides, spread disease
While cancer stalks the land, spread by human hand
Invading every home and womb.

Now, silent fields in all their greenness
Belie the treason of my kind against creation
Without reason, mere expedience and greed.
Now, genetically engineered seed
For livestock feed and virtual foods
Blight once hallowed land
Under corporate banners of progress, need
For which there is no redress.
Bodies, minds and spirits harmed
Spawn profitable drugs and services
As the Earth dissolves and humanity devolves.

December 2013

XXIII
Man Eating Dog

One must be very hungry,
Or really like the taste
To kill and eat a dog.
It might be out of dire necessity,
Cultural norm or sacred ritual.
But any way it brutalizes
Both the killer and the killed.

February 2006

XXIV
Dogs to Me

As an infant, I found every dog
A source of wonder and delight;
Responsive presence, a joy
To touch and eye to eye engage.

As a boy, they were my best of friends,
More trustworthy than my peers,
Incapable of betrayal:
More caring, playful, and aware.

To this dog-grown man, every dog
Is an open book to an open mind;
An open mind to an open heart;
A kindred spirit in canine form.

September 2010

XXV
My Dog Batman

You were my clock and pacemaker
Giving canine cadence to my every day.
For fifteen years, you got me up and out.
You knew the times to eat and sleep.
You were my compass needling me
Away from introspection to receive
Your unwavering affection so I in turn
Might give you undivided attention.
You shared my den and solitude,
My dreams and meditations.

I remember your wild cries of greeting,
Yowling yapping anguish and relief
From separation even brief:
The nuzzle of your cold nose against my palm
And pushes with your muzzle
To deftly place my hand upon your head
For me to touch and bless:
The earthy musk of your oval paws,
Flowery aromas in your perfumed cheeks,
And sweet hay scent where you had sat:
Your fastidious morning ritual
Of licking flanks, legs and paws
Then after face-washing like a cat,
Luxurious stretching on soft clean sheets:

Your trembling drooling jaws
Accepting treats so delicately
But anything new you always spat
To first inspect; instinctual wisdom
Of your scavenger lineage from poisoned streets.
Vivid still in memory your clear displays
To other dogs, of dominance, acceptance,
Playful intent. Shelties you adored,
Strange persons you would never trust.
You were never cowed or incautious,
Stepping everywhere with care,
Hidden springs in stocky limbs,
Your back-bouncing tail a gallant curl.
You always made me laugh

With your wiggle-dance and big grin,
You flashed my way
Just after you had pooped!

With age came the gray on muzzle and chin,
Your shiny lithe form more swayed, toes splayed,
Eyes grown clouded, hearing impaired.
Then more and more throughout the day
You slept; walks were shorter with no play,
Proud tail drooping with uncertainty,
Pointed ears flattening with pain and fear.
Slowly disengaging, fewer tail wags
And pushes with your nose as you strove
To close the distance for a moment
Until the gaze in your sad eyes returned.
It went through me and beyond
To tell me your time to leave was close.
When your appetite for food and life
Began to fail, and veterinary care
Was no avail, the time was right
For euthanasia's liberation because
You would rather stay and suffer
Than leave the ones you loved.
Now that you are here no more
Perhaps on some new, unfolding path
In different form, dimension,
The unbearable emptiness that you leave
Makes life around seem so unreal;
All feeling numbed by grief.
You will return in memory and dream
To kindle and affirm what we had shared
Love so strong I could let you go.
Little black dog Batman,
Rescued pariah from an indifferent India,
With the advent of your death, I feel
The mystery and wonder of your caste.
You were the enlightened one
For you have left your light
In my grieving soul to heal and hallow,
Illuming my way without you
Once always in my shadow,
Now, one breath away until I take my last.

In memory of Batman who left this life on 19 July 2011.
August 2011

XXVI
Sacred Elephants

In the racial memory of elephants
Long before the dawn of human consciousness,
Perhaps they, like us much later,
Recognized and revered a Buddha
Or a Krishna in their midst:

Appearing in their own image
Once in every millennium
To guide, inform, inspire,
Awakening them to the nature of divinity,
The divinity in their nature,
And the power of loving kindness.

If this is true for us,
Then their truth we share
To celebrate the sacred presence
That illumes our mortal lives.

Perhaps elephants are more enlightened,
Buddha-natured, Krishna conscious
Than we, a younger species
Beginning to evolve, recognize and revere
To save them from extinction
And all that makes us human,
Giving loving kindness to them all
And every creature great and small.

July 2011

(Poem published in the book, *Giant Hearts: Travels in the World of Elephants*, J. P. Puryavaud & P. Davidar, 2015.) Inspired by Heathcote William's book, *Sacred Elephant*.

XXVII
Consuming Innocence and Animals

Our collective taste for animals,
For their flesh and roasted fat,
Decorative skins and furs,
Prized hunting trophies,
Even potions medical and libidinal,
Casts a long shadow
Beyond their suffering and waste
Around the world, illuming
The hypocrisy of any claim
To love and care for fellow creatures:
Of being humane, even human,
Treating fellow beings as kindred spirits,
Not commodities and consumables.
Those who take the radical leap of empathy
Growing ever alien to their own kind,
The taste of flesh and roasted fat
Becoming the tang of pain and shame,
A revulsion that is not a sacrifice
But a renunciation before communion
And the healing of all our relations.

July 2013

XXVIII
What We Care to Eat

Where are the meadow larks,
The dancing hares?
Gone the way of wolves and bears,
And wild lands and wilderness
To grow the crops to fatten
Pigs and chickens in factory sheds,
And feedlot-cattle, sheep, horses:
Country sides industrialized
By appetites of indifferent greed,
By ignorance, not economy
And ecology defined.
Our appetite and our health
Are one, not gold and wealth.
Our appetites can change:
Restore the range, coyote sings.

Renew the countryside, larks wing
Above a recovering humanity
No longer squandering, consuming
Dreams of bears and children wild.

The call of wolf, hawk, whale
Is part of our communion,
Our spirits' food.
No more 'the cattle of the rich
Steal the bread of the poor'.
Our sustenance is a gentler fare.

Eating is a sacrament
Of Thanksgiving, gratitude.
The taste for goodness, wholeness,
Is a sense too few possess.
To adulterate or denature food
Is no less a sacrilege, a profanity,
Than to waste, allow to spoil,
Or horde for later profit.

We are what we care to eat.
Our forks are our fates.
Kitchen anarchists, caring farmers unite!
Our plates reflect the power of place,
With local foods, organic, whole
To mirror, nurture our humanity.

October 2009
Quotation from Mahatma Gandhi.

XXIX
For Deanna — An Ode to Stones

I had forgotten the songs of stones
Until you stilled my mind
And opened my heart's ear
To rock music in the rain
And their softer echoes under snow.

How different are their tones
In summer sun and winter ice.
How clear their choruses
In rolling river beds,
In mountain streams,
And their soft melodies
To mosses, flowers, trees,
Rooting in their essence.

What symphonies they sound
With different winds
That sculpt them smooth
With licking snails
Making perfect shells
And wind bells for gales.
Their crystal presence in my bones
Give me the power
Of an ancestry profound.
Thank you, Deanna, for connecting me,
And with Thou in all.

October 2009

XXX
The Way of Reverence

There are many ways of looking.
Those who look in reverence
See in a sacred way.
To see in a sacred way
Is love's gift to a world made profane.
There are many ways of feeling.
Those who feel reverence for all life
Know in a sacred way.
To know in a sacred way
Is love's gift to a world of pain.

There are many ways of living.
Those who live in reverence
Live in a sacred way.
To live in a sacred way
Is love's gift to a world made sane.

October 2006

XXXI
Nature's Hidden Truths

Victim, victor, opposing wills,
Predator, prey, survival of the fittest,
Nature raw, 'red in tooth and claw',
Men at war, compete, defeat.
Torn 'twixt discord, concord,
Might makes right for
Disconnected discontents
While lovers take the leap
Into unfathomed depths of otherness.

In every living presence,
We find a part of us abides
The *Inua* of the Inuit Eskimos;
The reflected image of some part
Of oneself in the eye, bark or pelt
Of every living other:
So when we care for others,
We are caring for ourselves,
As when we harm another,
We also harm ourselves.
Through all the strife and discord
Strings and chords of harmony
Spring from the wild heart core
Of the infinite, illimitable realm
Of all beginnings and ends.
They connect our souls and minds
With the unseen between
And within the seen. The peace
'Which passeth all understanding'
Then comes to Earth through us.
Weather, like our emotions,
Ranges and changes, nurturing,
Harming, annihilating, recreating
Beyond all love, hate, hope, despair,
Arising from the is-ness and it-ness,
Such-ness and otherness which abide
In the oneness of an eternal present;
An omniscient omnipresence
We feel in the first breath of spring,
Monsoon raindrops in the jungle breeze
Abuzz with wild honey bees
Before the hiss of distant galaxies

Sets the night air a-tingle to tiger ears
Beyond the clamor of our insanity
And Buddhist monks steaming snow
From their soul-ignited backs.

It is this miracle we live and breathe
Though joy and pain, forever blessed:
Forever healing, making whole,
Our hallowed Earth and home,
Sun swallowed, bright and beautiful
Until the next earthquake or tornado
As Shiva dances this cosmic cycle
And Pan still plays his pipes.

October 2009

XXXII
For William Blake

(Who raged against my homeland England's 'satanic mills'.)

'William Blake was no flake or fake.
He journeyed into the minds of men
Long, deep and very far,
Where some may weep, or rage, or sleep,
Or leap with joy and sing their star'!

Many rage with poet Dylan Thomas
Against the dying of the light,
But so it always must before the coming
Of the dawn, and each new age of man.

The age of peace is our release
From fear and hatred, vengeance, lust,
For all have trust and know the truth
That we are part of one stupendous whole,
Not man nor tree nor beast apart.
But no peace can ever be
Until every creature we set free.

Oh mystery! Oh majesty!
The awe igniting, reverence inciting
Wonder of the mind that senses,
Feels, and knows the wordless hymns
Of ancient trees and Monarch butterflies!

September 2009

XXXIII
The Falling Towers

I have seen how your towers
Of glass and steel,
Ephemeral, unreal, so transient,
Erected by unnatural, alien powers,
Scrape and pierce the sky,
Obliterate horizon's light
And blind the stars at night.

By day, they hum for mammon
As I feel the earth tremble, drained,
Your elevated state sustained.
Your shadow stain spreads pain and blight
Across the land you rent and rent,
Sucking the marrow out of life
Emptying souls' imagination
To accommodate profane creation,
Commerce, vital information,
Imperatives of global trade, control.

Towers of glass and steel,
Monuments to desire, inspire
A domineering state of mind
That sees a ravaged, vanquished Earth
As human progress; evolution:
Ingress to a world made new,
The promised land deserved and won
By a chosen few who claim their god
Made them in His own image
As they have remade the world
Into their own image, blind,
Unfeeling as their god,
To injustice, desecration.
Food from petrochemical-soaked fields
Courses through fetal brains without distinction.
Offspring of the rich play nihilistic computer games
With no countryside to run and find the wild,
Learn the names of things that feel and heal
Now obliterated by factory farms,
Silos for storing grain, nuclear weapons underground.
Acid rains kill ocean life, forests sickening,
Heralding the quickening of extinction.
The Hopis call this the Purification

Of Koyaanisqatsi, life out of balance,
For those living in the absence of the sacred
Who even spread and profit from disease,
Deny their role in climate change
And feel no pang across the range
Where buffalo and wolves once roamed
Amid the lush of prairie grass and singing larks.

I have seen the consequences of such dominion
For which there is no solution
Beyond my disbelief and outrage
Of this illusion of civilization.
Indigenous species, peoples disenfranchised,
Put in the zoo and reservation
In the name of feel-good conservation
To endure the poverty of spirit
Multiplying now in urban slums.

Every revolution in the name
Of freedom, justice and equality
Fails the test of evolution
When most within the towers
And those without
The ever multiplying minions
Of poor, oppressed, homeless, landless,
Whose leaders, political and religious,
Sanctify ever more violence and war
Feel, think, strive only for themselves.
Unmindful of the trees,
The oceans, and the least of these
Creatures from other realms, nations
Who express, embody and sustain
The life and beauty of the first world,
The original, the aboriginal.

The towers of glass and steel
Will all soon reel and fall,
Heralding their End of Days
As nature's powers defy,
Purify, restore and reify
The womb of life on planet Earth,
The First Creation,
Some future consciousness may cherish,
Hold as holy, sanctify.
The final solution lies in living mindfully
Of the countless ways we act
In the absence of the sacred,
To recover our humanity and sanity

Through reverence for all life,
Seeking peaceful co-existence
With all creatures great and small.
To walk in the grace of devotion
For all the beloved we cherish,
A consummation devoutly to be wished.

December 2012

XXXIV
The Way to Peace

We speak in many tongues,
but from what heart?
Hearts of love bring joy and peace;
Hearts of fear more hatred, war.
In freedom's name, some self-immolate,
take eye for eye and blind the world.
Suicide-bombers, kamikazes, martyrs,
victims, victors, tyrants, liberators
speak their truth from age to age
in many tongues. Now cyber-babble's
heartless language fills the world
while terrorists and religions intertwine.

Towers of babble come tumbling down.
Where are those who knew the language
of the trees and sang with whales and wolves?
They who know can show the way to peace:
Obedient always to the Golden Rule,
They live in grace on hallowed land
beyond the end of inhumanity
and births of empty souls.

Beyond the paradox of life in death,
Life gives to life, as we can chose.
Then peace will come
And all our slaughtering end.

July 2007

XXXV
Every Healer Knows

Every healer knows the Medicine Wheel
Is the Sacred Hoop the Hopis dance.
The drum-beat heart of Earth
Is in their feet, and eagles' wings,
As well the air we share.

Every healer, dancer, knows
The Hoop is broken now
But not beyond repair
If our will is in harmony
With the Power that moves us all
To care for the last of the wild
And the unborn of every kind.

Every healer knows to do no harm,
And in our healing of nature
Is the healing of self.
The drum-beat heart of Earth
Is in our feet, and eagles' wings,
As well the air we share.

March 2010

XXXVI
Forever Healed

Come join the Sun dance,
Call up the ancestors
Beloveds gone, mothers
Children, warriors, elders
Good dogs, horses, crows
Flying in on dream clouds
To dance around the Truth
With all of us, every love
And wound and wrong
Remembered, shared, atoned
Inside the circle around the Tree;
The scent of day, the Mother drums
To Fathers' feet in falling rain.
Kinship affirmed,
All relations* honored.

The covenant is sealed,
And all are healed,
Affinities sublime, illimitable.
Praying now, what lights
In many forms may come
To show and guide us
We thank and celebrate.

* With tree, and Thou, and thee and thy, and all on land, in sea and sky who crawl or swim, or fly or skim, or walk and talk, or pray and stay the sacred way. Dedicated to my Wailaki Indian friend, Ben Coyote.

January 2007

XXXVII
The Holarchy

(Where holarchists unite!)

The ethos of the natural world,
The law of nature, creation's code,
Is evolution or extinction; adapt or die.

Through the prism of culture, time and place,
Darwin saw in nature some primal hierarchy
Of competition and survival of the fittest.
Others used his vision as scientific proof
Of human superiority, and to justify the hegemony
Of industrialism and colonial imperialism
As natural human evolutionary progression
Biologically predetermined, if not God-ordained.

Kropotkin saw creative anarchy and mutual aid
That others warped into self-serving anarchism,
Paternalism, patriarchy, and mass-control.

Black Elk saw the Medicine Wheel,
The holists' vision of the holy,
Wherein all is sacred, co-dependent
As the web of life we each must hallow, heal.
He led his people to live in harmony
"With the power of the world as it lives
and moves and does its work."

Now under the chauvinistic monarchy
Of human domination, nature, animals
Are simply resources to exploit
Consume, abuse, transform.
The monoculture of the technocratic mind
Mirrors wastelands emptied of the wild,
Making inscapes of every child
Devoid of images nature made.
No imagination in an Earth un-souled,
Hominized, homogenized
By ignorant oligarchies of greed.

Evolve or perish, adapt or die,
The credo of creation long ignored;
Devolution unforeseen, progress mere illusion;

Virtual realities of *Homo technos*
Bereft of virtue, spirit, mystery.

No solution but dissolution
Without the Rx for evolution
Revolution in our ways of seeing
And of human being and becoming
In the holarchy of communion
With all sentient beings
And worlds within worlds.

Uncounted realms, spheres, orbits
Of existence, mind, action,
Spark our senses in the gravity
Of the draw of space illimitable.
The loneliness of our knowing
Consumes our lives unshared
Until we face the mystery
And embrace each other
In the certainties of death and night
To unveil the immortal nature
Of boundless love's unfettered souls.
Then alone like stars we shine apart
In radiance born to all unite
With constellations of harmony and peace
In nascent galaxies near and far.
July 2009
Dedicated to the late Thomas Berry who saw that "the universe is not a collection of objects but a communion of subjects".

XXXVIII
The End of the Race

Be of good cheer;
The end of the race is near;
The end of the human race.
I see only three riders left
In this mad human race
Ignorance, indifference and fear.

Power and arrogance, along with
Righteousness and retribution,
Began this biocidal surge.
Cleverness and cunning
Could not keep up,
And neither honesty and trust,
Nor morality, law and order.

Certitude and science
Helped lose the race
As the age of plenty,
After the age of reason,
Became the age of treason
Against nature, sanity and grace.

It will soon be over,
Nature will purge the race,
And in its place
Humility and compassion,
Devotion's sacred powers,
Will find their way
Into every human soul,
Imbuing all to heal,
Nurture, cherish and inspire.
How else to live
Within the cataclysms
Of cosmic wombs
And before the catechisms
Of sentient life
Throughout the universe
As undiscovered as the laws
Of nature's wisdom,
And the power of love
Inherent in us all.

October 2009

XXXIV
Evolve or Perish: A Paradigm Shift

"Physician, first heal thyself,
And do no harm,"
Hippocrates advised;
Let your medicine be your food
And your food be your medicine.
From *himsa,* harmfulness,
To *ahimsa*, non-harming
Is a paradigm shift:
A conscious evolutionary step
For *Homo* not-so-sapient man:
Biologically, a survival imperative.
Evolve or perish. Shift
From anti-bios, to pro-bios;
From antibiotics to probiotics:
From dysbiosis to eubiosis;
From warring against
To working together,
From humiliating to humility,
Making peace, not war
With weeds and bugs
Treating Earth as Mother
Soil her living flesh.
From humus comes humility,
And through our *metanoia,*
Empathy, and the humor
Of becoming one with the dance,

The dreamer of life,
And songs of stars and whales.

February 2010

XXXV
One Pilgrim's Way

Going to the ponds to explore their inner lives
Contained within their steep and muddy banks
The child found conscious life in a myriad forms
Within a world within a world of miracles,
The wonder and mysteries of all
Seeding wisdom, awe and reverence in his heart.

The boy collected with avidity and risk,
Pond 'specimens' for closer study, even retention
In his biological collection.
This natural science revealed Creation's art,
Nature's laws and poetry of life
Celebrated in blackbird's evensong
And the teeming wombs of ponds.
Other boys stole blackbirds' eggs,
Left blown up frogs around the ponds.

Adults drowned kittens in sacks
Threw in in their refuse
Then the ponds were land-filled
To build more homes,
Spreading suburban blight.
Nature out of mind and gone from sight.

Adolescent tensions between
The civilized and the wild,
The contrived and the authentic
Nascent in the natural child,
Tore him into two and for a while
He lost himself in others of the world
But not in it; aliens eating lambs,
Shooting wolves, making animals suffer
To find profitable cures for their own dis-ease.
Then the animals in his world
Whom he rescued, knew and loved,
Brought him to his senses
And the two became one.

The man raised and studied wolves
Finding the best and worst of human nature shared
But wolves more loyal to family and clan,
Superior stewards of the Earth

Living in accord with nature's laws.
He played with wolves who sang to his flutes
Making music in their bond of harmony:
Communion with the wild, vision quest of child
Completed, self-realized and affirmed
In the feral otherness and baptism
In nature's realm that blesses, nurtures all
Outside of temple, church and synagogue.

With a veterinary education, the man
Sought to heal the broken bonds
Between his kind and other animals
As well the living Earth they shared:
One World, One Health,
The medicine of the wolf.

He held his children high
To see the sky and stars,
Read the clouds and winds
Feel the rain upon their faces
To become what they were shown.
They too learned the love of wolves
And all the other animals who shared
Their lives and crossed their paths.
Drawn in his sunset years
To the essences of healing plants
He felt eternal gratitude for the gifts of life.
Before redeeming death's release
From suffering and mourning Earth,
Broken wings and falling trees.
He gave his last breath
To pray for his fallen race
To be restored to grace
Recovering compassion from extinction
By hallowing every living place
And all who dwell therein.

April 2015

XXXVI
For My Mother: In Memoriam

(Minnie Elizabeth Wilson Fox)

In my attentive father's shadow,
I remember how you helped me
Stand, walk, speak and spell;
Dispel childhood fears and fevers,
And explore the wondrous world
My senses sought to fill my soul.

Your delight in me reflected
My delight in every living thing:
Radiant crocus heralding spring;
Dancing butterflies, the laboring ant;
Blackbirds singing in the dell.

You preened my wings' imagination
To go beyond the speed of thought
Into what nature wrought and taught
A child becoming father of the man
Who sought to comprehend and care
For every creature of her creation.
As I was cherished,
So I came to cherish all.
Mother of every hue,
Inspired, enthused, embraced
The life around me and within,
I thank you for the gift of you.

You taught me courage and frugality
In the time of war with Father gone.
Only me to care for you with open heart.
The light of life you lived
And shared with all
Especially in your yoga classes
You gave till ninety-five.
Then close to ninety-nine
Your freedom came,
But the gifts of you remain
In all our hearts and souls.

September 2009

XXXVII
Our Animal Relations

Like many people grieving
Horses, elephants, and other animals
Have died from broken hearts.
Parent-animals will die
Defending their precious young.
None abuse, neglect their children
Like so many humans do.
Since when we first evolved
Animals have helped us, saved our lives.
More than we ever did for them.
Animals are not our inferiors
Or 'Created for man's use'
As one former Pope declared.
They are our relations
As genomics confirms
In wondrous form and function.
All sentient like us.

April 2024

XXXVIII
Help the Children

What do children learn in schools?
What inspiration, creative seed
Was sown in graduating fools
Who know nothing about
The forests and waters of life
No knowledge or experience
With beings other than human.
For most, there will be torments to come
From ignorance and indifference
To all our sacred connections and relations.
I wish for every child
To live with a rescued dog
Which will be possible
With open hearts and minds
When greed and poverty are gone,
Children no longer wrongly fed,
Becoming fat and sick,
The underfed, retarded, and diseased.
Save the children by having none
Or adopting one.
Give them bread before education
Then teach them about creation
Our Earth community,
Trees that give more to life than we.
Put co-creation before procreation
Learn to share and care.
We take better care of children
When we care for those of other species.
Help children play, discover mimicry
Becoming different characters, creatures
Shape-shifting bodies and minds
The way and wisdom of every shaman
Beyond race and gender, a moonlight bender,
Dancer, singer, music-maker.
Then they can let nature teach them
The ways of harmlessness and healing,
Wholeness and protection.

April 2024

XXXIX
For My Children

The longer I live
The sooner I will be gone.
There is no life without purpose.
Without purpose, I die.
So do not cry for me
When I am done
Because I found my purpose
In all you now embrace.
Living through the end of days
I wish you well; break the spell
Of anguish and despair.
Join those who care
To make new days come
For all you cherish, heal.

July 2024

XL
That God Be Damned!

Creatures sing in oceans deep
Others touch me in my sleep.
Eagles let me feel the sky.
Others in my dreams I cannot heal.
I cry.
My childhood's sense of awe and wonder
In the presence of any other
Who was not human
Are now shadowed by all the plunder
Not seeing other as brother
Kindred spirits harmed by our inhumanity.
I awake remembering all the cruelty, suffering
I have witnessed to document and stop.
The Boundless Circle, Sacred Hoop, is broken.
Compassion can repair when more can feel
And be renewed by singing birds and wolves,
Saved from the cultural insanity of a collective
Psychosis of superiority, of God-given dominion,
With all the animals created for man's use.
I say to that god be damned!
The God of nature and nature of God
Are indivisible but not invisible.

July 2024

XLI
Trees of Life and Wisdom

I breathe in trees,
And feel them breathing me.
I think as trees,
They teach me many things.
Reverence is all I can return.
We breathe together as one breath.
Standing trees making clouds,
Drawing rain, holding the hills
Making rivers clear and pure
Standing in trees in rain,
Dreaming hillsides, rivers like branches.
Standing in trees I learn sun dances,
Seasoned, ancient, cadences
With the Earth's axis keeping time.
Standing like a tree I know
A different time, original, complete,
Where my body finds its aboriginal roots:
Roots turning rocks to life,
Matter into spirit, evermore;
Evermore until the axe and buzz-saw.
They hack your living limbs
In the wholesale devastation
Of your ancient groves and forests
By people who have lost their sense
Of sacred time and place and being,
They have no roots, no memory
Of their place among the trees,
Transforming matter into spirit.
They go against the grain,
For selfish gain, so ignorant

Of will divine that lives,
And moves and breathes in all
For all, and not for them alone.

August 2024

XLII
For Deanna: On Our Wedding Day

Assis, Italy
20 May 1987

The swallows of summer's return
Make macrame songs in the air
Above the mad cities and ruins
Where the flesh off our bones is dust.
We will fly with the swallows, Deanna
And knowing their songs of delight
Can soar beyond cities and ruins
To dream the world back to light.

XLIII
The Delta Sphynx

How many men have loved you
Yet love was not enough?
How many men have seen you
Between this realm and the next,
Seen beyond desire and wonder
Solving the riddle of you
Gazing into eternity
Sphinx of the river sands?
How many hands have touched
But not felt; how many eyes
Have looked but not seen
Beyond their own desire and wonder?
The answer to the riddle is the river.
Like your soul it cannot be contained,
Possessed. It must be free
And like the river you must move on
Form lover to lover
Until the river ends
Not in death, though so it seems
But in the union of I-Thou
Of sea and river meeting at the delta.
There is our peace sublime
That passeth all understanding
Until it is experienced.
Only though such love is the riddle
Of the delta sphynx resolved.
Neither nemesis nor apotheosis
But both for each of us,
Two halves made whole
In the gnosis of one heart's
Eternal embrace.

May 2023

XLIV
For Deanna: In Memoriam

We shared the best and worst of times
Through weariness, joy and grief.
Now you are gone, I find relief
Kindling the light of you
In all the work I do.
I shall not retire.
I find you in your things I touch,
See you always in everything.
You still inspire, once helped me focus,
Banishing unmindfulness and hocus-pocus.
How I miss your flame and fire!

July 2024
Deanna L. Krantz, 6/17/1949–12/27/2023

XLV
When I Write and Why

Words pour out of me
In an endless thread
A dreamtime stream
Giving me a life-sentence
In love, sorrow, outrage.
I do not know and dread and vent
Numb beyond the endless flow
Of words entangled in despair
That so many never care or see
Or feel for wildness in a cage
Billions in crowded factory farms
Soon to be killed by bloody arms
For someone's thoughtless meal
All consumed without a thought;
Others suffering to find the balms
For those diseases, they could prevent
Or poison every infestation
Regardless of their own procreation.
So, I write, fight the unnamed
To let every soul be free.
Lions doing tricks in the circus ring
Applauded, our dominion lauded;
Caged canaries with no sky still sing
Spirit of hope not yet terminated.
Whales harpooned, wolves exterminated
Dogs and elephants chained
Beasts of burden beaten, maimed,
"Put all heaven in a rage."
I strive to preserve my sanity
With sound science, ethics, reason,
Against the might of inhumanity,
Where animal protection is for naught,
Environmental protection fought,
The covenant broken, the treason
Of our sacred duty to care and to heal
A ravaged Earth and every relation.
I will continue to compose